*The wild geese do not intend to cast their reflection;
The water has no mind to receive their image.*

> – Chuang Tzu

THE
ONE
IN THE
MIRROR

Yogi Impressions

Yogi Impressions

THE ONE IN THE MIRROR
First published in India in 2004 by
Yogi Impressions Books Pvt. Ltd.
61, Anjali, Minoo Desai Road, Colaba,
Mumbai 400 005, India.
Website: www.yogiimpressions.com

First Edition, September 2004

Copyright © 2004 by Ramesh Balsekar

ISBN 81-88479-11-X

Printed at: Thomson Press, New Delhi

Foreword

I remember that evening vividly. It was during the seminar in December 2003, that we were relaxing on the terrace of the Rockholm Hotel overlooking Kovalam beach. The sun was low on the horizon, behind Ramesh, its rays scattering jewels on the sea.

Ramesh told me that for some time now, he had been writing small passages which came to him spontaneously. These had accumulated and could now be compiled into a book. I loved the idea of such a book. One you could pick up any time, turn to any page at random to read a couple of passages, and then put it down to let their meaning sink in. In this age of information overload, it was a brilliant way of conveying the teaching.

You will find no chapters in this book, as we have endeavored to retain the spontaneity of the writings as they happened – in an 'unbroken wholeness', as it were. These reflections are from a man who has had an illustrious yet simple life – as a family man, bank president, a leading Advaita sage loved by people across the world, and a prolific author of over 20 books. At 87 years of age, I could think of no one better 'qualified' to present these gems of understanding to guide us on our life's journey.

The basic concept of Ramesh's teaching that there is only One Source pervades the entire book. No one is a 'doer' but, rather, all actions are happenings ordained by this One Source. As Nobel Laureate Pablo Neruda wrote: *When did smoke learn to fly?*

Ramesh's guru, Nisargadatta Maharaj, said, "The same mirror that shows you the world as it is, will also show you your own face." May this book serve as 'a polishing cloth'.

Gautam Sachdeva
August, 2004

Preface

The mirror as an object of divine intervention is timeless. Its efficacy is delightfully recounted in the ancient myth of Shinto Japan:

Terrified by the violent acts of her brother, the beautiful sun-goddess, Amaterasu, recoiled into a heavenly rock dwelling. As darkness descended, the universe was threatened by an inevitable end. Faced with calamity, the counsel of gods advised that a mirror be placed opposite the entrance of the cave. A simple but ingenious plan.

The forlorn Amaterasu, amazed and enticed by a fleeting glimpse of her own magnificence, gently stepped forth. When light was restored to the world, the gods rejoiced and stretched behind the sun-goddess a rope of straw, called a shimenawa. And though Amaterasu may retreat each night into a restful sleep, the shimenawa ensures that she does not disappear forever...

What, one might ask, is the relevance of this story to a book of reflections?

A reflection is none other than a mirror, a plane of wisdom in which we can at last truly see ourselves. Imbued with pure, spontaneous insight, this book sparkles with a luminosity that beckons us out of our dark and solitary confinement into renewed vistas of eternal light. A light that is peace, a light that is harmony...

Protected within the bounds of an invisible shimenawa, amidst fields of meditative contemplation, we are free to meander with the innocence and careless abandon of youth. Knowing that we shall never be lost again. Guided by the silence of sunshine. Reflections mirrored in the flow of life.

Anjali
August, 2004

We are not the reality, not the substance, but only its reflections, its shadows: the substance is there in the moment, in reality, hidden from us by the screen of time.

Purpose Of Life

The purpose of life is to watch life happening. I can watch life happening only if I am anchored in peace and harmony from moment to moment. I can be anchored in peace only when I am not uncomfortable either with myself or with others. I am not uncomfortable only when I do not hate anyone, either myself or the 'other'. I do not hate anyone only when I am able to accept totally that "events happen, deeds are done, but there never has been an individual doer of any deed."

Transformation

Any deep understanding, any transformation, can happen only in a still mind, only in that alert and yet passive mind in which there is no blaming, no condemning, no conflict, no resistance. In such a state of mind, one is simply confronted with 'what-is', which is precisely what is supposed to be according to the Cosmic Law.

Harmony

In the end, all happiness can be reduced to three words: 'me', the 'other', and the 'relationship' between the two. If the relationship is harmonious, there is happiness. If the relationship is unharmonious, happiness is absent.

The One Source

The Source can only be One – the Unmanifest Unicity transforming into the multiple manifestation. It is this impersonal energy, functioning through the human psychosomatic apparatus, which generates the original thought leading to individual action. This is considered by the separate entity as 'his' action. Thus, the whole process of the individual entity with volition, considering himself the doer, is in fact the activity of this impersonal primal energy.

As the *Rubaiyat* of Omar Khayyam puts it:

> "With the Earth's first Clay They did the
> Last Man's knead,
> And then of the Last Harvest sow'd the Seed:
> Yea, the first morning of Creation wrote
> What the Last Dawn of reckoning shall read."

This Impersonal Energy is the one source of all the opposites in the manifestation, beginning with male and female. From the human perspective, the cosmic drama appears as a play between the inter-dependent polaric opposites of every conceivable kind.

As the *Tao Te Ching* says:

> "Under heaven,
> all can see beauty as beauty
> only because there is ugliness.
> All can know good as good
> only because there is evil."

'I Am'

The Source does not need to be aware of Itself.
Awareness happens – *I Am* – as the Impersonal Awareness
in manifestation. When the 'I Am' identifies itself with
an object, the personal awareness arises as an individual
object.

Conflict No More

Living one's life involves a series of happenings in
which an awareness of the 'me' as a separate entity really
does not exist. The 'me' becomes conscious of itself only
when there is conflict. Until then, so long as everything
is moving smoothly without any frustration, without any
contradiction, there is no consciousness of oneself in
action. I am aware of myself and my 'problem' only when
I am blocked by something that the 'other' has done which
has affected me adversely.

It is necessary to understand the relationship between
'me' and the 'other'. Normally, if I am hurt or opposed,
my immediate reaction is that the 'other' has done it
and so I hate him. If, however, I am able to accept that in
life, as the Buddha has so clearly stated, everything is
a happening and nothing is a deed done by anyone, the
'conflict' simply cannot arise. If I am hurt, it is obvious
that the event – according to the Cosmic Law – was
supposed to hurt me, and, most importantly, through
which body-mind organism it happened is totally
irrelevant.

Freedom For The Ego

The basic problem of the ego is whether what is sought is freedom *for* the ego or freedom *from* the ego.

It is quite clear that a sage has to live the rest of his life, after he has had the full Self-realization, as the same separate entity that he was before. How then can he say that he truly sees no separation between himself and the 'other'? There is the problem! How can the ego – which is identification with a particular name and form as a separate entity – be destroyed and yet live as a separate entity?

In other words, it is obvious that a sage continues to live his life as a separate entity, and, therefore, he must have an ego. How can there be an ego without the sense of separation? Such a contradiction it seems cannot have a solution, and yet there is a simple answer. The sage *does* see a separation between 'himself' and the 'other', but only as the separation between two separate instruments, through both of which the same energy functions and brings about whatever is supposed to happen according to a Cosmic Law.

When the sense of personal doership is thus removed from the ego, what remains is only the identification with a name and form, a totally harmless ego, a mere instrument through which life happens. It is the sense of doership that causes the meaningful separation and, when that is destroyed, no real separation exists.

The freedom that is sought is really not freedom *from* the ego, but freedom *for* the ego from the sense of personal doership.

Orbit Around Reality

At the end of the day, if one sat quietly and reviewed the events of the day, not as separate segments but as one whole totality, one's perspective could be astonishingly different. One would then see the whole not as a series of causes and effects but as a totality that is not the totalization of fragments seen one at a time. Our perspective would then not be separate judgments of separate segments based on human logic and human standards of fairness and justice, but the Totality based on the Cosmic Law.

Indeed, the perspective could change very radically: that we ourselves, the shadowy egos, are in movement and what we observed as events of the day was the immobile. Like planets circling round the sun, like electrons round the nuclei of the atom, our life and living would then be an orbit around Reality. This would be totally different from seeing life like a split-second vision of only a slice of Reality which we stretch into a continuity like a cinema film made up of still, individual frames.

And, of course, the review could be over a day, over a year or even over a lifetime. The only obvious way would be to let the body-mind organism react to a life situation in the moment according to its natural programming, otherwise it would mean the ego making a judgment continuously on each segment every moment, and never on the totality of Reality.

A Transitory World

How can we know that the world is transitory, that time is passing, that nothing stands still? We cannot know that our river is flowing unless we have one foot on the bank! There is no entity, only a continuum*, and that continuum is Consciousness.

Silent Light

Meditation – Relax totally and sink into the silent light of impersonal immortality.

Understanding What-is

Truth ultimately can only be the understanding of 'what-is'. 'What-should-be' is only a concept based on desire, and one desire is continuously replaced by another. It is only in a state of mind free from conflict, passive and yet alert, that the intention to understand the Truth in 'what-is' can exist. The actual position at any time, unfortunately, is that we are constantly seeking methods and systems. However, it is only in the spontaneous tranquility of mind that there can arise the real understanding of 'what-is'.

* continuum – a continuous sequence in which adjacent elements are not perceptibly different from each other, but the extremes are quite distinct. Origin Latin, from *continuus* 'uninterrupted'. – Compact Oxford English Dictionary

How Does Consciousness Occur?

It seems that scientists are seeking clues about how the subjective inner life of the mind arises. A true understanding of the phenomenon of consciousness remains elusive.

How do the brain's physical systems work together to create the subjective experience of the mind – the self-reflective, private thoughts that make us what we are? Noting the difficulty of using empirical science to quantify something so subjective, David J. Chalmers, a philosopher at the University of Arizona, has dubbed this as 'The Hard Problem'.

Neuroscientists can outline which functions the states of consciousness fulfill and which physical, chemical, anatomical and physiological conditions are necessary in the brain for the development of these states. Yet, they would still be left with the critical question: how does consciousness occur? For now, no definitive explanations exist, but the scientists hope that eventually the mysteries surrounding consciousness will fall away in the face of persistent scientific enquiry.

Could it not be, however, that the problem itself is misconceived?! That something so subjective as consciousness cannot be 'created' by any neurological process at all? Could it not be that the very essential basic core center of every conception that occurs is itself consciousness? The problem itself would then dissolve.

Contentment

If God came to me in my dream and asked me what I wanted most in life, I would ask for a state of mind in which I would not have to ask for anything: peace of mind... contentment.

Surrender

How does a spiritual seeker seek? Every time he comes across a sentiment, statement or concept that fits in with his inherent programming – genes plus conditioning – he adopts it enthusiastically, while at the same time ignoring with contempt those which he did not like or, more frequently, did not understand. This process continues with fervor as his jigsaw puzzle builds up, until he has a personal patchwork of concepts that has no real significance at all. Such a progress could never in a million years produce the essential understanding that the initial urge has been obliging him to seek.

What we are required to do is exactly the opposite of this: to 'lay down' absolutely everything that is 'ours'. Naked, empty-handed, we must go to the Guru in all humility, and then the Guru will remove the accumulated 'ignorance'. What the Guru will reveal to us is the One Whole, immutable, though couched in various concepts. Gradually, what seemed difficult to understand will get clearer, until finally, all at once, the entire meaning will become manifest, and we shall *know* the ultimate understanding.

Past Conditioning

There is no question of the necessity and utility of knowledge as such in daily living. 'Knowing how' kind of knowledge is absolutely essential in dealing with situations in life. But the knowledge constituted by psychological beliefs involving fear, desire, security – the past conditioning – acts as a hindrance to Truth.

What Am I Seeking?

For the seeker, the basic question should be: what am I seeking? If the answer is enlightenment, what will it do for me for the rest of my lifetime that I did not have before?

It is because this is not addressed, either by the Guru or the disciple, that such enormous frustration is associated with spiritual seeking, ending with the feeling that it is all illusion and hypocrisy. Enlightenment has to be found in the very living, and not considered an ideal or principle of perfection, which as such can only be an escape from life. The real question, therefore, is whether it is possible to live daily life in a state of enlightenment with a sense of greater ease, a sense of fulfillment, which the ordinary person does not have.

What the ordinary seeker expects is something positive: *ananda* – joy, bliss. And this is what has been held out to him, all these years, as the carrot before the donkey. Which doctrine, which system offers more, is the usual choice before the seeker.

From my experience, I would very clearly tell the seeker that I do not know of any positive joy or bliss which does not very soon give way to misery and pain. All I would hold out before you is *negative gain*: if you are able to accept totally, without the slightest doubt, that all action, without exception, happens as an event which has to happen at that time and place, through a particular body-mind organism, according to God's Will – Cosmic Law, and is not an action done by any individual human entity, then that is enlightenment.

What is the benefit of this enlightenment to the individual entity for whom this has happened? Very simply, since he is not doing anything at all, nor does anyone else either, he goes through the rest of his life without the slightest load of shame and guilt for his own actions and without any hatred and malice towards any other entity. A state of negation – that is all. And yet this state of negation is the very basis for peace and harmony: to be anchored in tranquility while necessarily facing life from moment to moment.

Jivanmuktas Of History

Ramakrishna Paramahansa, Ramana Maharshi, Hui Neng – the outstanding, incontrovertible examples of men who lived, each in his own way, for long years in a state of illumination, in a state of freedom from living itself. None was at any time an intellectual. Each spoke as a separate entity from the plane on which he lived, in that time, in that culture.

Their 'verbal formulae' differed, but the sense of their words is amazingly identical. They were speaking precisely of what they knew from their experience. Their words do not excite controversy or arouse in us an expression of opinion. They go straight to our hearts like stones thrown into a pond.

Besides the words of the *jivanmuktas*, what is the value of the theories of the metaphysicists and philosophers who write about something they seek and hope to find? These are obviously necessary for discussion amongst students, for teachers talking to students, but let us not forget that these are merely opinions and theories, interesting and stimulating though they may be.

It is, of course, a fact that an intellectual approach could lead to the necessary intuitional approach. But do we truly know of any man, historically speaking, who realized the Truth through a strictly intellectual approach, merely through studying the Vedas and the Upanishads?

The Experience Of Oneness

Some people have an experience – sometimes more than one – of Oneness. The background and the nature of the people differ on a very wide scale. It seems that there is no minimum 'qualification' for the happening of an 'experience'.

The usual effect of such an occurrence is that the experiencer keeps wanting a repetition of it, and quite often becomes frustrated. What then could be the significance of this kind of an experience? The only relevance would be to bring home to the experiencer the basic fact of life – that it *happened*, that it cannot be something that could be achieved.

Such an event emphasizes that nothing in life, no pleasure or ecstasy, can ever match the bliss of Oneness that happens when the body is dead and the ego has vanished. There really can be no individual 'experiencer' at all. Therefore, the only thing to 'do' is to be still and let life flow, without giving too much importance to any pain or pleasure in the moment. Finally, death is not something to be feared but welcomed.

What Happens After Death?

You are concerned about what would happen to you after death. There is no need. What will happen to you then is precisely what had happened to you before birth. There was no 'me' to be concerned with anything before birth, nor will there be after death. The dream that started with birth will have ended with death.

Don't worry, be happy, live your life moment to moment!

13

There Is No Creation

"There is no creation, no dissolution," said Ramana Maharshi. "From the beginning nothing exists," said Hui Neng, 1300 years ago.

Scientists like Louis de Broglie and Schrödinger appear to have demonstrated mathematically – and in the laboratory – that there is nothing real that exists, nothing absolute that could exist: "Mass appears to be only resistance to change (to movement of energy), decreasing in bulk in accordance with acceleration and increasing proportionally in energy. In other words, matter has no existence as such."

Wise men, with intuition, have believed Ramana Maharshi and Hui Neng. The others will believe the scientists.

Only A Reflection

In living our lives as separate entities, being in control of our lives and responsible for our actions, 'we' are but objects pretending to be the Subject.

'We' are not the reality, not the substance, but only its reflections, its shadows: the substance is there in the moment, in reality, hidden from us by the screen of time.

Our 'life' in manifestation is a continuous mis-apprehension by which a shadow is mistaken for the substance, a reflection for its image, an echo for its voice.

Total Listening

I do not ask my visitors to accept my concept, but rather, that they listen to what I have to say directly and not through the screen of their accumulated tradition, habit, prejudice, beliefs, desires, cravings, and fears. All I ask is that they listen totally and then test my concept in the fire of their own experience.

Discovering The Self

What exactly is Self-knowledge? Self-knowledge cannot happen by sitting in a corner meditating about myself. I exist as an individual entity only in relationship to people, things and concepts. I can only know myself by watching, observing, studying my relationships, as well as my inward thinking. Anything else would be an abstraction. I must study myself as I am, not as I wish to be.

All I need to do is simply observe in the mirror of relationship my attitude regarding people, things, ideas, and concepts. Without judgment, without approval, without condemnation. That very perception turns out to be the action, the beginning of Self-knowledge.

Self-knowledge is not a process of accumulation. It is a process of discovery, not of judgment, in relationships. It means observing the ways of the mind, how one looks at neighbors, how one treats people one likes and does not like. All these things are like mirrors in which can be seen one's real self and, if one is alert, one is astonished to discover everything anew from moment to moment.

Receptivity

The mind that is capable of insight, intuition, must necessarily be free from all accumulated knowledge, tradition, superstition, escapes. Only then can there be receptivity, resonance to what is being heard. And then we shall be free: an attitude of detachment from the accumulated baggage will result.

Self-improvement

J. Krishnamurti tells us that: "the self becomes extraordinarily important with the idea of self-improvement." At this point, a valid question arises. Should one not try to improve oneself? There is great wisdom behind this statement, and it behooves us to find out what he had in mind.

One dissipates loads of energy in the conflict between 'what-is' and 'what-should-be'. The ego is unable to face 'what-is' and projects a 'what-should-be' as an escape route. This is what Krishnamurti tells us to avoid. He asks us to face the 'what-is', and investigate whether the 'what-should-be' is valid. When facing the 'what-is' one has to be totally honest: this means forgetting one's conditioning as a Hindu, a Christian, a Buddhist, and facing the 'what-is' as a total human being, the total consciousness. And then there is the greater possibility that there never was a question of 'what-should-be'.

Integrally Intelligent

Knowledge, as such, can be a definite impediment to the understanding of Truth. When one says 'I know', it simply means one has information – recognition of a fact or an experience one has had. The constant accumulation of information, the acquisition of various concepts, all constitute the assertion 'I know'. When you analyze it, investigate it carefully, you will realize that the very assertion 'I know' is in effect a wall separating you from the 'other'. Behind that wall, you have sought comfort and security, and thereby made yourself less capable of receiving the understanding.

The question really is whether it is possible for the mind to be free from accumulated information and belief that keeps us enclosed and incapable of resonating with the outside. One who is earnest about discovering the Truth has to face the problem of knowledge and belief, applied equally to religious and philosophical concepts, and also the expertise of scientists, technicians and reformers.

To think from a conviction or a conclusion is not to think clearly at all. A mind that can be receptive and open to the Truth must necessarily be free of the conditioning of a set of beliefs. For coming out of the prison of one's own making, there is an obvious need of a deep intention to understand, not just an idle curiosity. It is only if we are able to put aside the heavy baggage of information and beliefs and concepts, that we can expect to have the freedom of a still mind. The deep wanting to understand brings about the stillness of the mind: there is absolutely no effort, no conflict involved, in the understanding. There is a distinct feeling of relief from the burden of striving for something, but the mind is not dull; it is simply quiet without any pressure to be still.

When the mind is free from the influence of the past,

then in that seeing there is transformation – Truth – in which knowledge plays no role. Wisdom – Intelligence – Understanding arises when knowledge with its continuity ends.

Knowledge, however wide and deep, does not necessarily indicate wisdom: the sensitive awareness of the totality of life – its problems, miseries, contradictions, the entire gamut of interconnected, polaric opposites which are the basis of life and living. It gives us expertise in limited fields, but it fails to make us *integrally intelligent*, totally aware of the whole process of life.

Images Of The Mind

The relationship between every 'me' and the 'other' – the very basis of life and living – is based on the image-forming defense mechanism. Each of us builds an image of the 'other' and of ourselves, and it is these two images that interact, not the human beings themselves. Our perception is not only with the senses, but also with the thinking mind, which is heavily conditioned. Thus, intellectual perception is only partial, and all of our relationships imaginary.

It is only when we truly understand this that there is the possibility of the absence of any conflict... a sense of universal brotherhood. This means a total acceptance that every human being is a helpless, uniquely programmed instrument through which life happens according to the Cosmic Law. Then alone can there can be love between 'me' and the 'other'.

Intervals Between Thoughts

It is so very necessary to clearly understand the 'intervals between thoughts'. They are *not* brief glimpses of a world surrounding us, or messages from such a world. Thoughts arise in the conditioned aspect of Consciousness. It is Consciousness that shines clear in the interval between thoughts.

Such intervals reveal us as we are: we then know ourselves as Pure Consciousness. It is precisely to this realization that we have to awaken from our living-dream.

We tend to believe that intuitions squeeze through the thought-intervals, from somewhere or the other, and reach our brain or our mind – our cognitive faculties. This is the nonsense of identification. These between-thought flashes are moments when we are ourselves. Thoughts arising in the conditioned aspect of Consciousness are related to the dream-figure with which we are identified.

'Intuition' – looking within – is really looking *from* within. Intuition is our impersonal 'Self' and, when we recognize this, we become it for the duration of the apprehension. The awareness of thoughts is 'we-as-Consciousness', but then they are our objects, whereas intuitions are subjective and Consciousness itself. The 'interval-between' is pure, impersonal 'I'.

Freedom Of The Moment

When some work is being done, of whatever nature, you are in the freedom of the moment. When trying to get something over and done with, you are in the bondage of horizontal time. In the former, it is the working mind functioning; in the latter it is the thinking mind.

19

Vertical Mind

What the ordinary man does is 'horizontal' living with his self-doership. The sage, with an ego that has totally lost its sense of personal doership, lives 'vertically'. The 'vertical' is 'real': the 'horizontal' is 'unreal'.

Non-attachment, non-abiding, non-conceptualizing, non-daydreaming all mean living 'vertically' instead of 'horizontally'. Intuition is an expression of the 'verticality' of mind. The 'vertical' mind is always present – in the present moment. The 'Kingdom of Heaven' is the 'vertical' mind.

Enlightenment means turning over from the 'horizontal mind' to the 'vertical mind', from the objective direction to the subjective.

There Is Only Seeing

Without seeing, the object does not exist. 'Seeing', 'experiencing', signify the cognition of all forms of manifestation. They indicate 'pure perception', which is subsequently interpreted as the apparent universe. There is only 'seeing', 'experiencing'. There is neither the 'seen', nor the 'experienced', neither the 'seer' nor the 'experiencer' – both are interpretations of a movement in Subjectivity, which is termed 'see-ing' and 'experience-ing'.

Neither before nor after see-ing, experience-ing, is there a see-er, an experience-er.

Quietness

When true seeing happens without a 'me' as the observer – without the image, without the opinion and the judgment of the 'me-observer' – one suddenly recognizes something that is extraordinary: the silence of the mind, the purity of what is observed. And this quietness is not something that can be cultivated. It is the result of deep, profound attention to 'what-is'. This extraordinary gift remains until the 'me-observer' returns and smashes the gift to smithereens.

An Eternal Present

Every sense perception is, in itself, obviously spontaneous, impersonal, instantaneous. It is in the present moment, the only present we can ever know. However, as soon as the perception occurs that we, as the subject, have perceived the object, as soon as intellection has taken place, the present has already gone because the intellect cannot operate on anything that is not already past. Intellect can feed only on dead meat. The living perception is slayed by the act of cognition.

It is only our memory that creates the past. It is only our desire for something, or our fear about something, that creates the future. In other words, we only know the past and imagine the future. Does the present ever exist for us? It is always a memory before we can conceive it. We have only to think for a moment: the past can only be a trick of memory based on which recollections differ, and the future only a fabrication for the fulfillment of desire. Can there really be anything other than an eternal present – the present moment?

Waking Reality And Dream Reality

In a dream, we are aware of 'me' and the 'other'. We feel anger, fear, compassion, pleasure, pain. We think and exercise our reason. Whatever is taking place is indeed happening 'out there' in the world around us. But when we awaken, we realize that it was 'only a dream', a creation of the mind.

The sole difference between a dream and the waking reality is that while the dream experience was based on memories, hopes, and other such factors, the happening in the waking state is based on sensory information drawn from physical surroundings. This gives our waking experience a sense of reality which is lacking in our dreams.

The fact of the matter is that our waking reality is as much a creation in our mind as our dreams. There is no basic distinction. All experiences are an image of reality *created in our mind* – whether in the waking state or in the dream state.

Burden Of The Past

We have often been told of the great advantage of being in the *now* – the present moment. The only way this can happen is if we are rid of the burden of shame and guilt for our own actions, and the burden of hatred and malice for others' actions. To be rid of this burden is to be able to accept absolutely that "events happen, deeds are done, but there is no individual doer thereof."

Screen Of Time

Many scientists have confessed that the answer to a problem which made them famous came to them from out of the blue, 'from outside', as Einstein said about the equation $E = mc^2$. A similar breakthrough has to happen to a spiritual seeker who knows he has the total intellectual understanding of a crucial concept, but is equally certain that it has not become *total*.

What is 'beyond', out of the blue, the 'outside'? Undoubtedly, it is a further dimension screened from us by our self-made concept of 'time'.

A phenomenon is something that occurs in three-dimensional space interpreted with the fourth dimension seen serially as time: Reality is motionless, ubiquitous, permanent. The fourth dimension when seen by us serially as time, as opposed to its total aspect which is eternity, produces the illusion of manifestation – *maya*. What seems to us to be serial – cause and effect – is really in eternity fixed and permanent. What is seen as a movie, frame by frame, is actually a film already produced, and already in the can.

A stone thrown at a ceiling fan will pass between the blades if the fan is not working, or is working at a slow speed, but will be rejected if the fan is in full motion. The blades are clearly visible when they are not in movement or when the movement is slow, but as soon as the movement becomes faster, they become invisible. This is because the human eye does not react with a rapidity sufficient to seize the moving image. If the rapidity of the reaction of the eye was increased, or the movement of the object retarded, the blades again become visible. Artificially, of course, this is done in photography: the shutter of a camera can be operated at a greater velocity than the reaction of the eye.

These so-called 'laws' could apply to our perception of time, on the basis that the 'outside' is separated from the 'inside' by the screen of time. If we could speed up our perception, or slow down the psychosomatic apparatus, we could make contact with what is 'beyond'.

Our whole lives are bound by time. We can hardly perceive sensorially without coming against the limitation that is time. Our senses, however, cannot traverse it because its frequency is too high. We now accept the speed of light, regarded as the ultimate velocity by relativity, perhaps only because we can experience no higher.

The screen of time is impermeable only in certain conditions, as in the case of a sieve. Just as many things can pass through the blades of a fan, from bullets to light, some elements can pass through the screen of time, such as intuition or a flash of acceptance, presumably because of a higher frequency than thought or logical reasoning.

This means that if an adequate readjustment of frequencies could take place in our consciousness, if the rapidity of our time apparatus decreased or the rapidity of our perceptions increased, we too should be able to apperceive Reality (not just perceiving the Reality but something transcending the perceiving) and become sages, with the covering of *maya* totally removed.

The Play Of Life

The purpose of life is to witness the Divine Will functioning through the many body-mind organisms as *lila*, the play of life and living.

Time Is Movement

If we imagine life were to 'stop' for a perceptible moment, what will have happened? Time will have stopped. Therefore, time is movement. But time, as Kant has said, is "a function of our receptive apparatus." Therefore, any movement can only be within ourselves. When we 'die', movement stops, and life remains 'immobile' – eternal in its permanent state.

Who Is Really Moving?

If we are in a stationary train and another train arrives alongside and stops, both trains are stationary for a while. And if then one train starts, we really cannot know which of the trains is moving. We may think we are moving and the other train is stationary, or it could be the other way around. Similarly, we think we are still and the future comes to us, becomes the present moment, and then becomes the past. Could it not be that what is happening is that the entire existence is unmoving, immobile, and it is 'we' – the illusory, shadowy 'me's' – who are moving around it?

All There Is, Is God

Simple people want to see God as if He stood there, and they here. But the fact of the matter is that all there is, is God. Who is there to see him? The moment I feel truly that I am nothing, all there is then is God.

If God came to me in my dream and asked me what I wanted most in life, I would ask for a state of mind in which I would not have to ask for anything: peace of mind... contentment.

Essence Of Meditation

Meditation is not traversing along a path leading to an imagined bliss of some sort. Meditation actually happens when the mind watches the flow of life, seeing and listening without opinion, without any judgment, wholly attentive to the movement of life in all relationships. This could happen throughout the day, not necessarily when you sit in a particular posture trying to stop the movement of the mind by various means, internal and external, such as controlling the breath, reciting a mantra or counting the beads of a rosary. The essence of meditation is watching the movement of life in relationships without judgment.

Equanimity

To be enlightened is to be able to accept with equanimity anything in life at any moment as God's Will.

The Present Moment

The present moment is only an imaginary division between past and future – like the equator between the two hemispheres.

Neither existing in *samsara* nor not-existing in *nirvana*, we are not anything in any way that we can *know* ourselves, except as the present moment.

Life Happens

I accept nothing, I reject nothing.
In any given situation I watch decision and action
happening, together with the consequences.
Sometimes there is pleasure, sometimes pain.
I find myself sometimes watching what happens:
Life is a TV serial.
Sometimes walking, sometimes resting.
Sometimes thinking about things without conceptualizing.
I do not have to know that I am happy!

Be Aware

Go to sleep with the awareness that you may never
wake up; wake up with the awareness that life can end
any moment.

Let All Things Be

Do I have a message for you? Yes. Let all things be
precisely as they are; love them and be kind to them as
if you were the Creator.

God Is Great

"God is Great" does not mean He is greater than
something else – there is nothing else at all. It means
that He is too great to be seen by the eyes, and too
deep to be understood by the intellect.

Humility

Genuine humility is that which is not recognized as such by the one who has it.

No Pleasure Without Pain

What is life for the human being? Seeking more and more pleasure. Fun! *Always* wanting our own little corner to be safe, peaceful and enjoyable. The human being seeks pleasure without realizing the basic fact of life, namely, that there cannot be pleasure without pain.

Our psychological background makes us behave like animals tethered to a post. What we are really looking for, whether we know it or not, is to be free from psychological conditioning, which makes us excessively concerned for our well-being. What a joke! This seeing itself is the end of our seeking: seeing without the chains of knowledge and craving.

Cage Of Conceptualizing

We are so concerned with our own worries, hopes, and desires, so preoccupied with personal problems, so heavily burdened with beliefs, traditional routine, with the past or the future, that we shut ourselves in a cage of our own conceptualizing, and are unable to either truly see or listen. It is this lack of attention and intention that has made ineffective and inconsequential the teachings of those who have transcended the phenomenal barrier and have attempted to describe for us the path that they have traversed.

Enlightenment And Innocency

I was once asked by a visitor: "Ramesh, are you enlightened? And what did you achieve through enlightenment?" I found myself answering: "I don't know what you mean by 'enlightenment', but I would rather use the phrase 'ultimate understanding'. What is my ultimate understanding? It is that everything is happening according to a Cosmic Law; no individual can be the doer of any deed. What have I achieved? Only the understanding that I cannot blame anyone for 'what-is' in the present moment – neither 'me' nor the 'other'. This means that, whatever happens, I cannot hate myself or the 'other'. The understanding has given me total freedom from hatred. And absence of hatred means the presence of peace with myself and harmony with the 'other'. That is what I have received from the understanding."

When the visitor heard this, there were tears in his eyes and he responded with the words: "I am really deeply impressed – not so much by what you precisely said, but by the utter innocency with which it was said."

For some time afterwards I thought about the spontaneously used word 'innocency'. I suddenly remembered that it was used by J. Krishnamurti, who wrote: "One must be alone, but this aloneness is not isolation. This aloneness implies freedom from the world of greed, hate and violence with all its subtle ways, and from aching loneliness and despair. To be alone is to be an outsider who does not belong to any religion or nation, to any belief or dogma. It is this aloneness that comes upon an innocency that has never been touched by the mischief of man. It is innocency that can live in the world, with all its turmoil, and not be of it."

Innocency means the total acceptance of 'what-is' and not comparing it with any 'what-should-be'.

Life Being Lived

All Masters have asked that everything has to be 'laid down', forsaken – conditioning, knowledge, science, religion, self. Actually, the most important, perhaps the only potent thing, is the idea that one lives his own life, whereas actually one's life is being lived.

We do not choose to be born, choose to grow old, choose to be ill, or choose to die. How then can one imagine that we choose anything in-between?

If we can 'lay down' our stupid and arrogant notion that we live our own lives volitionally, we shall have let go of everything all at once, *en bloc*.

'Horizontally', we can have no freedom whatsoever. 'Vertically', there is neither freedom nor non-freedom.

The Original State

When the ego continues to believe in its volition and personal doership, it means clearly that the ego cannot accept its nothingness, with the result that it continues to be liable to sorrow, antagonism, insecurity. What the total acceptance of non-doership does is to remove the various accretions that the sense of doership has accumulated. Without this burden, which has led to the load of guilt and shame towards oneself, hatred and malice towards the 'other', the ego realizes its original state. The experiencing of this nothingness means peace and wisdom.

Looking At Oneself

Has one ever looked at oneself as if one were not the 'me'? Truly looked at oneself without choice, without judgment, without evaluation? Next time you are shaving or brushing your hair, have a good look in the mirror. What exactly is happening? 'You' are not shaving or brushing your hair. A psychosomatic apparatus, a body-mind organism, is doing something. Let the impersonal looking continue and what will be seen is not someone doing anything, but the doing *happening* through a human robot. This is what happens when there is real looking, not so much with the eyes as through the mind and heart. Then there is a kind of explosion, a sort of mutation, that brings about a real transformation or revolution: "Events happen, deeds are done, but there is no individual doer thereof."

Detachment

It is a simple fact that it is necessary to detach oneself from the limitations of habits imposed by our three-dimensional conditioning, so that one can be open and receptive to the fourth dimension.

Detachment is not the totalization of *achieved* affective indifference. The suppression of pride and arrogance, desire, anger, or whatever cannot destroy their cause: a disease cannot be cured by suppressing the symptoms.

When the personal doership and its affectivity is transcended, all its manifestations automatically disappear. Only by understanding the falsity and futility of the affectivity of personal doership, upon which the ego depends for its sustenance and strength, can detachment happen.

Tranquility

The human mind is an intriguing phenomenon, with its unsteadiness and its lack of stability. Even when no activity is going on, the mind is not still: it is thinking about the past and the future. Even with eyes closed, we keep seeing images and entertaining ideas about persons, things and events. The mind is like a machine that is working all the time. Apart from its restlessness, it is always engaged in a conflict between opposing urges and desires. This restlessness of mind is closely related to the sense of personal volition and doership. Once there is the conviction that there never was a thinker, only thinking – never was a doer, only doing – only then does an emptiness arise in the mind which leads to tranquility and peace. Truth.

Attraction And Attachment

Money has always had a peculiar attraction for me. As an early seeker, I used to worry about it. And then, later, I understood the basic difference between 'attraction' and 'attachment'. Attraction happens because of the programming in the body-mind organism – genes and conditioning – over which the ego has no control at all. Attachment is wholly a matter of the ego and its involvement.

I have had the sneaky suspicion that my attraction for money is based on the fact that as a school student I had no 'pocket money'. There never was a shortage, but it was given only for a specific purpose. It was when I joined college that I had some money of my own – merely the monthly amount of scholarship. Although this is just speculation, the fact of the matter is that attraction in itself need not be a worry for the spiritual seeker.

Thinking Mind Is The Villain

"The sun is new each day" is one of the most penetrating maxims of Heraclitus. It is the thinking mind – the aspect of the mind that dwells in the past and continuously projects into the future – which prevents one from seeing that the sun *is* new each day.

Each morning is new, each pleasure is new, each pain is new. It is the thinking mind that is old. It is the thinking mind, the mind of accumulated memory, which prevents one from living moment to moment, out of the inner harmony of the here and now.

Life for any individual human being means a relationship with the 'other'. The 'other' represents everyone else. The whole problem of life is that one looks at the 'other' through the mind of accumulated memory of guilt and shame for one's own actions, and hatred and malice for the actions of the 'other'.

Existence is always in the present moment: fresh, moving, a dynamic force, a dialectical movement, flowing like a river, not something stagnant. If one is able to take life as it happens, without the thinking mind, its memories and hopes, one would always remain young. Young in spirit. Even death will seem a great adventure, a culmination, a door to infinity.

Knowing The Mind

To know oneself means watching one's behavior, one's words, one's reactions in everyday relationships. To know the mind is to be aware of desire and fear, of guilt and shame, of hatred and malice.

Space And Silence

Our conditioned thinking makes us consider silence as the polaric opposite of sound and suggests that the prevailing silence is broken by new sound. On the contrary, silence is to the ear what space is to the eye. Space is not broken when an object is observed in space; nor has silence been broken by the arising of sound. Each sound is surrounded by silence which continues to prevail when the sound disappears.

What is even more enlightening is the fact that both space and silence exist in manifestation, the silent space of Pure Awareness. The creative emptiness of Pure Awareness is realized in correct perception when we see that emptiness is the potent no-thing-ness around which the storm revolves, and which enables the wheel to turn around its axle.

From this perspective, meditation – true meditation – is being in the silent space of Pure Awareness. It is not a way to enlightenment for the ego to follow, nor is it a method of achieving anything at all.

Selective Awareness

We usually do not have the experience of Pure Awareness because we are only aware of those events, things, facts, feelings that stand out from their background. If there is no discrepancy, nothing unusual, then it does not register in our mind. There is no awareness in the normal course of being in good health; the mind only notices the condition when our health is impaired in some way. Our conditioning then continues unnoticed, and the burden of past accumulations continues unabated.

Awareness And Attention

We would see the basic difference between 'awareness' and 'attention' in the fact that awareness is what is inherent in all experience, and yet it escapes our attention quite easily.

Our brain works in such a way that we cannot pay attention to something without at the same time ignoring something else: we see the movie but ignore the screen, we pay attention to the printed word but ignore the page, we see the stars and ignore the space. We cannot pay attention without ignoring something, and this needs effort. Awareness is the non-dual noticing of both the ignored and the not-ignored. It is the most natural, impersonal happening in which the 'me' is absent. Whereas attention is personal, in which there is a 'me' paying attention.

Space will not be affected in any way by breaking a clay pot that contains space and at the same time is contained in space. Similarly, when any object in the manifestation is broken, destroyed, or dies, awareness cannot be affected in any way. One is thus the living Awareness – never born, never living, never dying – from which everything arises and into which everything disappears. Awareness includes both the interconnected opposites of every conceivable kind and all possible opposites in any situation.

Awareness is aware of all that arises without the slightest effort: it accepts nothing and rejects nothing.

As Chuang Tzu put it:

> *"The wild geese do not intend to cast their reflection;*
> *The water has no mind to receive their image."*

Objective Reality

The human being feels deeply that he is able to accept anything as true if he is able to see it: actually, he means if one of his senses confirms it. He can only be aware of that aspect of the manifested universe of which his senses are able to inform him.

A man without sight is less aware of the universe than a man with sight. An animal, a psychosomatic apparatus like man, having only five senses, has percepts without concepts, and is not likely to be aware of his psyche. As oriental psychology has always held it, a man has a sixth sense in as much as he is aware of his mind.

To imagine that the universe is limited to that of which we can be aware of is as unfounded as the perception of the universe to an insect with only one sense, his antennae. That which is darkness to us is not darkness to the cats, while what is darkness to the birds is not darkness to us. On the scale of smell, many animals have a much wider range than that of human beings.

To the extent that our senses have a wider range than that of many other creatures and a more limited range than some others, we do have experimental evidence that the universe can be more or less restricted than the one we are supposed to know. And, of course, to the extent that our perceptive ability in relation to the universe is extremely limited, the objective reality of the universe as such – assuming there is such – must remain forever as unknowable to the human being as to the microbe. This should be a very humbling thought.

Passive Awareness

What is meditation must be clearly understood. It is not doing an exercise with the object of achieving something. This contains the seed of desire. True meditation, which can bring about a transformation, a real understanding of oneself and an astonishing degree of peace and repose, is that in which there is no process of concentration on any object or desire, but rather a passive awareness of every thought and feeling, without any involvement or judgment of any kind.

Meditation is not a seeking, or an exploration, or an investigation. It is neither a matter of keeping the brain or mind in control, nor is it supposed to be a 'self-introspective analysis'. In such an exercise there is a constant tussle going on between concentrating the mind on a fixed point while the mind keeps wandering off. Such a conflict can be avoided only by being passively aware of all thought as it happens, without any resistance or opposition. Out of that awareness of the entire movement of one's thought, arises the awareness of one's being. A total absence of the personal 'me' as the individual doer that opens the door to creative happening.

Let Life Flow

If you set out to meditate, it will not be meditation. It will be an exercise of some sort. If you set out to be good, goodness cannot flower. If you cultivate humility, it can only be inverted pride. Let life flow.

Perfection is attained not when nothing more can be added, but when nothing more can be taken away. When an image is being hewn out of a piece of stone, the sculptor keeps chipping away until he cannot cut any more. Then the image is ready.

True Meditation

How does one meditate? True meditation is when there is no meditator doing meditation with the object of achieving something. The 'method' may be different.

An eight-year-old boy, sitting in meditation with his father, when asked, said: "I take myself inside myself and think of God." Ramana Maharshi said: "Seek the source of thought." My own method is: "Surrender into the nothing. That is all there is."

Realize Your Nothingness

Knowing what you are exactly – your good points and your bad points, together making up your nature – shows that this 'you' is the programming in the psychosomatic apparatus and not really you. You are, in fact, nothing. Though unaware of this emptiness, you, the ego, can only come to this inevitable conclusion after investigation from your personal experience. What you thought was your action was in fact a happening, the result of another happening over which you had no control.

Without the sense of personal doership, you, the ego, realize your nothingness, and then the ego-mind becomes still. In this tranquility, the nothingness becomes the vibrant truth without any encumbrances.

Criterion For Values

If I earn 3000 rupees a month, and after the usual expenses I can save only 100 rupees, a gift of 1000 rupees could be seen in two ways: one-third of my salary or ten times my monthly saving. What we tend to forget is that money is not the first point of exchange: it is an intermediate point. Even as one is struggling to earn money, one is exchanging a part of one's life for it. Pursuit of money can become an end in itself and destroy all sense of values.

When you buy a new house or car, you can consider the cost in terms of what price you have paid, or, more realistically, in terms of how large a portion of life you had to expend to acquire it. Likewise, one's occupation could tend to become the sole pre-occupation until acquiring money becomes a way of life, thereby distorting one's sense of values. The only way to live a sensible life is to have a sensible criterion for values.

Love And Hate

The injunction is: Love everyone. I would be satisfied with a simpler one: Do not hate anyone – neither yourself nor anyone else.

Agreement

One of the most important things in life is to accept disagreement without being disagreeable.

The Real Beauty Of Meditation

Meditation does not have any root, nor any substance which the mind can grasp. In fact, perhaps the most important aspect of it is the absence of any desire to possess anything. There is nothing that must necessarily happen in meditation every time: sometimes it can be deep beyond imagination, while at other times it is extraordinarily light like a wafted breeze. It is this unknown factor that is the real beauty of meditation: there can be no expectation at any time. Sometimes, one sits for about an hour and it seems like half an hour; sometimes it could be the other way around. There is really no question of any meditation as having been good or bad, successful or unsuccessful.

What We Are Not

The only method of recognizing that-which-we-are is by recognizing that-which-we-are-not. This means that all we have to do is to apprehend that we are *not* anything that our intellect has been conditioned to assume in its interpretation of sensorial perceptions. By knowing what we are not, we are left with the understanding of what we are.

A Pure Heart

What has Self-realization given me for the rest of my life that I did not have before? A pure heart! This in turn has provided the foundation of peace and contentment while facing life, accepting whatever each moment brings – sometimes pain, sometimes pleasure.

Discipline

Discipline etymologically means 'learning'. Is there really any sense in laboring to remove the manifestations of the ego by 'discipline'? Effects disappear not when they are repressed or suppressed, but only when the causes are removed. Understand deeply that everything is a happening according to the Cosmic Law, and not the doing of any deed by anyone. Demolish the false sense of doership in the ego, and the manifestations of the ego will disappear by themselves.

Ego Must Remain

Many Masters have clearly stated that the ego is the enemy and must be destroyed before awakening can take place. I have always had difficulty with that statement. How would the sage live the rest of his life as a separate entity without the identification with a particular name and form? The answer, of course, is that it is the *sense of doership* in the ego that has to go.

Freedom?!

Bondage, Liberation – what are they but words?
I am the infinite Self, the witness of everything happening.
Whether through this body-mind organism or through another.
Thus I am free of all guilt about my actions,
And free of all hatred for the 'other's' actions.
What do I need 'freedom' from?!

It Is An Illusion

It is an illusion, a fantasy, a mistake, to think we live our lives.

It is quite clear that our lives are 'being lived'.

It is an illusion, a fantasy, a mistake, to think that we control and manipulate events; actually, we are controlled and manipulated by events.

It is an illusion, a fantasy, a mistake, to think that we perform one action after another; actually, an endless series of actions – one action after another – creates 'us'.

As a child once said in anger when asked by his mother to stop sneezing: "But, Mom, I am not sneezing – it is sneezing me."

Security And Permanency

From the time a baby is born and seeks its mother's breast intuitively, seeking becomes the very essence of living. The human being is always seeking: seeking a purpose in life, a goal for living, seeking satisfaction, pleasure, safety, security.

There is an all-pervading feeling that one is missing something. One almost feels as if one is being cheated of something that is one's birthright. So we try to fill that void in ourselves, that incompleteness, that emptiness, that loneliness with various ideas and concepts, ultimately resorting to seeking a permanency that we give various labels, including 'God'.

We are seeking endlessly and we do not know precisely what it is that we are seeking. We want a replacement for our parents to protect us. We are overwhelmed by the insecurity of life. However, the basic question is: security and permanency for whom? For the 'me'!

For Self-knowledge to come into being, the only solution is to be found in the understanding of the 'me'.

Mirror Of Relationship

In the mirror of relationship – between you and your family, between you and nature, between you and your thinking – you will see yourself clearly: your feelings, your motives, your urges, your fears.

It is a discovery to see yourself as you actually are, not as you think you are: impatient, quarrelsome, greedy, envious, and often stupid. It is important to observe the fact without either trying to justify it or trying to alter it. This is indeed a wonderful revelation.

Relationship With The 'Other'

What kind of a relationship do I have with the 'other'? How can I have contempt or loathing for anyone if I have accepted totally that one's personality is determined by programming – genes and environmental conditioning – over neither of which has there been any control? How can I hate anyone if I have been able to accept that every deed is a happening and not something 'done' by an individual? When I cease to despise the 'other' for whatever the reason, the reaction can only be compassion.

Whether you like someone or not depends on your programming. But if *dislike* prevails, it is the ego judging. This is a clear distinction and not merely a play on words.

Harmony In Relationship

The basis of life and living for 'me' is my relationship with the 'other'.

I can never hope to have peace with myself unless my relationship with the 'other' is harmonious. There can be no harmony if there is an underlying feeling of suspicion and fear of the 'other' as someone who could cause me harm. The only way I can never have any such fear is if I am able to embrace *totally* the concept of the Buddha: "Events happen, deeds are done, but there is no individual doer of any deed."

This can happen only if I am able to accept that the 'other', like me, is an instrument through which life happens, from moment to moment, according to a Cosmic Law. Thus, it is not the 'other' I have to be afraid of, but my own destiny. If it is not my destiny to be harmed, no power on earth can harm me.

Therefore, when my relationship with the 'other' is clean and pure constantly, it will rub off on the 'other' too. And then, of course, the harmony has become mutual.

Friend Or Foe?

Whether friend or foe, understand and accept the combination of good points and bad points. Beware of the bad points and support the good points, and very soon you will turn a foe into a friend.

Men And Women

I recently came across the incident of a married woman who had the compulsive need to leave home, husband, and an eight-year-old son, retire to an ashram and devote herself to social work. It was not just a whim, but a persistent wanting that made life hell for a whole year. The husband and the child were understanding enough to accept her unusual need and let her go. Since then I have wondered if the situation would have been different if the woman wanted to leave home with another man.

The Arabian sage, Monoimus, says: "If you want to feel one with God, find out whence is it that you wake up when you would rather not, fall asleep when you would rather not, fall in love when you would rather not." Perhaps he might have added: "...and fall out of love when you would rather not."

The relations between men and women do present a mystery about which they seem to be wondering all the time. They have a constant need for one another, and yet rarely do they seem to understand one another. There usually seems to exist a state of unceasing conflict, almost latent enmity, between them. On analysis, this conflict seems to be based on a struggle for domination. The obstacle that lies between them is the ego with a sense of personal doership, perhaps the urge for possession.

But, truly, we have never possessed anything – we never could. What is there to possess? And who is there to possess anything? And for how long? The process of 'living', in time and space, is an illusion. *We are*, but our living on the plane of existence is wholly illusory.

On the material plane we have certain rights and obligations according to certain laws. We can possess, by law, a house, a garden, a car, even a wife, and on the same plane we can dispossess ourselves of such articles and rights.

49

No human being can 'possess' another. Human life is essentially lonely: an old bachelor is no more lonely than a young one; a bachelor no more lonely than a man with a wife whom he dislikes; a man with a wife whom he dislikes no more lonely than a man with a wife whom he loves; a man with a wife no more lonely than a man with a harem.

The only man who is not lonely is the one who is forever in harmony with the 'other'. And the only man who is in harmony with the 'other' is the one who has, by the grace of God, been able to accept that everything *happens* – according to the Cosmic Law – and is never the deed done by any individual entity.

When men and women accuse one another of disloyalty, it is almost every time a question of fact, and a fact is, on examination, found to be false, exaggerated or almost always misinterpreted. It should suffice to understand, instead of to misunderstand, suppositions. The only fact is that one was able to suspect the 'other' of disloyalty. This means that he or she projected that evaluation from him or her onto the 'other'. Loyalty is not a thing-in-itself but something integral in 'love'. And disloyalty is as unthinkable in love, as breathing without air. Illusory evaluations shut out spontaneity, the living present moment, in which any relationship really exists.

Masculinity and femininity, the two interconnected aspects of a single manifestation, are in a state of imbalance, each manifesting an excess of one element. The association of the male and female has the apparent effect of restoring this imbalance to a state of equilibrium. This mutual attraction of the male and the female, and the need of each for the 'other', becomes comprehensible because the attainment of equilibrium would seem to be the goal sought throughout the functioning of manifestation.

What can be attained in life, however, is never the real fulfillment, but only a simulation of it, resulting in sexual experience on the one hand, and conflict on the other. But in some rare cases, contact between male and female may constitute a union on the plane that is beyond the comprehension of our senses. Such a contact could more accurately be described as 'force-fields'. The more dynamic and less impermanent example of this phenomenon could perhaps be called, not too accurately, 'love', as witnessed in the relationship between Ramakrishna Paramahansa and his wife Sharada.

Ancient Wisdom

A great philosopher in Greece was asked two questions:

Q. What is the most difficult job in the world?
A. To understand oneself.

Q. What is the easiest job in the world?
A. Preaching to others.

The Vedas tell us:

Donate with kind words, donate with happiness;
Donate with sincerity, donate only to the needy;
Donate without expectation: it is not a gift, it is a duty.
Donate with your wife's consent;
Donate to others without making your dependants helpless;
Donate without caring for caste, creed or religion;
Donate with an intention that the receiver should prosper.

The Gift

If I give something to somebody, or help someone to obtain or to do something that he wants, am I doing him a service or myself a disservice? Am I gratifying the fictitious self of that person or affirming my power over him? Am I gratifying my own fictitious self and increasing its pride and arrogance?

I distinctly remember the occasion when I offered a substantial gift to my Guru. When he accepted it, after making sure that I could really afford it, I felt a sense of gratitude for his giving me an opportunity to deprive myself of something, thereby weakening the stranglehold of my fictitious self.

Gratitude And Forgiveness

If, as Buddha considered, the total acceptance of the fact that events happen according to a Cosmic Law, and no deed is ever done by an individual entity, is the ultimate understanding, then the two words *gratitude* and *forgiveness* lose their significance.

When something good happens to me, it is because it is my destiny according to the Cosmic Law. Whom am I grateful to? If I am hurt, it is my destiny to be hurt. Through which body-mind organism an action happens which hurts me is totally irrelevant. Whom do I blame and whom do I forgive?

True Love

For the average person, *love* is a manifestation of the violent, possessive doership of the ego. Whereas for the spiritual person, it is not a sentiment at all, but a state of mind in which love exists to the degree in which the selfish element is transcended.

According to the average person, the desire for possession is the criterion, the touchstone of sincerity or reality by which love is to be judged. Even the mother is accused of not loving her child if she is not particularly possessive towards her baby. Love – the sentiment, and love – the non-affective state of mind, where a subject-object relationship does not exist, are infused by the same force. Though basically not different, one is steeped in egoistic involvement, the other unaffected and pure. The former is exemplified by the love of a man for a woman, the latter, sometimes called divine love or *caritas*, is a luminous pool of light and not a beam focused on one object at a time. All-embracing, bathing all alike in its radiance.

It must, however, be recognized that the discrimination between spiritual and romantic love is illusory because both are aspects of the same reality. Physical expression of love cannot be excluded because the relationship is on the plane of phenomenality. In a few rare cases, even the sense of doership and possession will not exist.

Recently, I came across an instance where the personal element was not excluded from true love. A nurse recounted: "While taking care of my patient's wound, we began talking, and he told me that he needed to visit the nursing home to eat breakfast with his wife. She had been there for a while, a victim of Alzheimer's disease. I asked him if his wife would be worried if he was a bit late, whereupon he replied that due to her loss of memory she no longer knew who he was, nor had she recognized him in five years. I was surprised and asked him: 'And you still go every morning?' I had to hold back tears when he smiled, patted my hand and said: 'She doesn't know me, but I still know who she is.' I realized that *true* love is neither physical nor romantic. True love is an acceptance of all that is, that has been, that will or even will not be."

Illusion Of Perfection

Perfection in life and living is really an illusion because the basis of manifestation is duality, interconnected opposites or polaric counterparts of every conceivable kind, beginning with male and female.

Everything will have its opposite. How can there be *perfection* when there can be no beauty without ugliness? Acceptance of this fact, that his own body and personality has both good points and bad points, means humility in the sage accompanied by tolerance for the 'other'.

A Mask For Pride

True humility is the inevitable condition arising from the annihilation of personal doership and the absolute acceptance of the Buddha's words: "Events happen, deeds are done, but there is no individual doer thereof." Otherwise, humility can only be a mask for pride, its counterpart.

Learning Through Experience

It is so very necessary to distinguish clearly between a thought that arises over which no one has any control, and the horizontal thinking that may result thereafter.

The arising of the thought is something no one can prevent. What results as a reaction to that thought which has happened vertically in the present moment, is thinking in horizontal time. Such reaction is based on the vestiges of past experience, and will vary widely according to such conditioning. In other words, the same thought in different psychosomatic apparatuses would produce varying responses by way of horizontal thinking. These vestiges of past experience are referred to by various terms such as 'the known', 'the accumulations', 'the past', 'the conditioning', but they all mean the knowledge and experience we collect in life. Bertrand Russell has called this process of association as "learning through experience."

It is a curious fact that we are not usually conscious or aware of the process of learning – the process of experience – we have gone through since childhood. And, therefore, the meaning and significance one reads into various events and happenings are actually the result of one's habit formed unknowingly. All one's thinking is based primarily on conditioning, over which we have had no control.

The psychologist, A. Gessell, has described the development of the 'self' in a child as follows: "Up to eighteen months of age, the child is self-engrossed but not self-aware, since he does not very clearly recognize the non-self. At two years, he begins to use self-reference words – 'mine', 'me', 'you' and 'I' in that order. At three years of age, the idea of 'persons' becomes clear. At five and six, the child begins to see even in terms of individual qualities."

Total Energy

Real silence of the mind can only happen with Self-knowledge: to be quietly aware of the ways of the mind, to be fully aware of its subtleties with their implications – to be aware of the 'me-observer'. The 'me-observer' lives in fragments – one thing in the office, another at home, yet another at the club and a totally different one when he is alone – full of guilt and shame, hatred and malice.

The point is that we have rarely looked at ourselves, hardly ever. We are afraid to do so. The usual way is that of escape, to try to explain things away, to blame others. It is only when we are able to accept totally that whatever happens in life is not something done by anyone, but an event bound to happen according to a Cosmic Law, that all fear, contradiction and conflict disappears. Life then becomes a matter of such awareness as to exclude nothing. Such awareness is total energy, in which state of attention the totality, the nakedness of oneself, is at once revealed. This is Self-knowledge.

Basis Of Conflict

Truth can never possibly be anything other than 'what-is'. There is conflict only because one does not accept 'what-is' and creates the idea of 'what-should-be'. To be more accurate, Truth is not 'what-is', but the understanding and acceptance of it. Any running after 'what-should-be', based on concepts, can only be an escape from 'what-is'. There is no complexity in 'what-is', but only in the various escapes – religions, concepts and beliefs.

Facing The Problem

The problem in life is usually the relationship with things, people and concepts. We always seek a solution to the problem, and there never is a solution! All solutions are based on concepts and beliefs. What is really needed is very simple: to face the problem and not to escape from it. Just seeing the truth in this fact is often enough: seeing that the problem does not exist in the absence of a desire of the 'me-self' seeking the fulfillment of that desire. In that split-second is seen the Truth, the 'what-is', revealed to a mind that is capable of facing itself without identification or any belief. Only personal experience can bring about acceptance. The seeing is the only doing necessary.

Ultimate Understanding

The Source, Energy, Self, Consciousness, God – by whatever name we understand It – is necessarily *One*. The One, in its expression, has become the many in its phenomenal manifestation. In the functioning of the manifestation – life as we know it – everything happens according to the Cosmic Law.

What is one expected to do in a given situation in life? Whatever one thinks one should do. What actually happens will be according to the Cosmic Law.

Aloneness And Loneliness

There is a basic fundamental difference between being lonely and being alone. Throughout the history of mankind, what we find is that excessive self-concern, self-occupation, is the outstanding feature of human behavior. Human life is anything but a matter of certainty, fulfillment, plenty. On the contrary, life is like an obstacle race.

We can see that our whole activity is self-centered. We keep thinking about ourselves endlessly: we must improve ourselves; we want a better job; we must fulfill ourselves; we want a better relationship; we want to achieve enlightenment. Our self-concern motivates all our activities. It is this pre-occupation with the self and rivalry with the 'other' which brings about isolation and loneliness. We try to escape from it in various ways, but such strategies cannot succeed.

When one is conforming to a pattern – religious, psychological or even self-imposed – there is bound to be a contradiction between 'what-is' and the pattern. The self becomes supremely important with the idea of self-improvement. One needs tremendous energy to see this situation in its truth and entirety. It demands utter honesty to recognize that 'what-should-be' is an avoidance from the actuality of 'what-is'.

It is only the urgency to see the truth, that can make us accept the 'what-is' in the present moment. One needs to be completely alone in this investigation. The accumulation of conceptual knowledge must be totally set aside. And such aloneness certainly does not mean isolation: it does not mean building a wall around oneself. On the contrary, this means one is *not* alone but represents all humanity, a universal brotherhood, regarding all separate selves as merely instruments through which the Primal Energy – Consciousness –

functions and brings about, at any moment, precisely that which is supposed to happen according to a Cosmic Law.

It is only such an awakening of Divine Intelligence which ends selfishness – the cause of loneliness of the self.

Be Not Afraid

One day, a visitor – a teacher in a junior high school in Germany – said she had an irrational fear of any group of people. When I asked her if she also felt fearful in her classroom, where there was always a group of 'others', her answer was that, no, there she was in control!

This, I think, is the very basis of why the relationship between 'me' and the 'other' is not harmonious. The 'me' is afraid that he or she is not in control: the 'other' may not do what the 'me' wants, or may do something which the 'me' does not want, and truly hurt me.

The situation will change only if it is totally accepted that what happens to 'me' is entirely my destiny – God's Will, Cosmic Law – and has nothing to do with the 'other's' intention or action. If it is not my destiny to be hurt, no power on earth, no 'other', can hurt me. Why be perpetually afraid of the 'other'?

I may not be in control of my life, but the comforting knowledge is that no one else can control my life either! It is entirely a matter of the Cosmic Law.

Spontaneity

Non-action can also be usefully called spontaneity.

Children Over Graduates

Here is an interesting riddle, the correct answer of which was provided by 80% of kindergarten school children and by only 17% of university graduates.

What is it that is greater than God and more evil than the devil, which the poor have and the rich do not need and, which will kill you if you eat it?

The answer is 'nothing'.

Uncertainty In Life

Uncertainty in the future is the basis of life and living: no one can know whether the next moment will bring pain or pleasure. Unless one is able to accept this fact *totally*, living will be a continuous frustration. It is not possible in life to hold a seat in the 'reserved' compartment, nor to escape from this fact.

What one seeks is freedom from this fear. However, the most important thing is that this seeking is not a process in time. It is not acquiring any knowledge. What is needed is wisdom, intuitive intelligence, *to see clearly the problem itself, not the solution.* Seeing the problem intensely leads to dissolution of the problem.

The fear of the unknown is obviously created in the mind. Such fear cannot exist if the mind is silent, unoccupied. The thinking mind, based on the individual self, is usually obsessed with creating fears and hopes for the future. When the mind is empty, unenforced, and there is no horizontal thinking, in this state of mind there is no thinker, and in the absence of the thinker, there is no fear. There is all the needed action when the mind is totally still, no longer seeking escape.

Positive And Negative

When the fifth Zen Patriarch felt the need for a successor, he asked the members of the sect to write a brief epitome of the doctrine.

Shen Hsiu, the leading member of the sect, wrote his famous lines in a beautiful aristocratic script, stating that the body is like a *Bodhi* tree, the mind like a bright mirror, and that we must keep that mirror clean and allow no dust to settle on it. This is the typical positive doctrine: the mind – Consciousness, Awareness – being likened to a mirror yet again, a vast, imperishable reflector, whose purity must be maintained for it represents Reality.

Hui Neng, a young, illiterate peasant, whom the fifth Patriarch had working in the kitchen, got someone to write for him the same number of lines, stating that there never was a *Bodhi* tree, that there never was a bright mirror, that from the beginning nothing ever existed, and that, therefore, there was nowhere for dust to alight. This is the negative way.

The positive doctrine is a long path because the 'me-concept' as a pilgrim is led astray at every turning, and is pushed over the precipice at the very end.

The direct path is the negative way, along which no 'me-concept' can travel, for a shadow cannot travel by itself. It means direct seeing by cutting horizontal thinking – conceptualizing and objectivizing.

Beauty Of A Silent Mind

Hardly anyone is aware of the beauty and wonder of a really silent mind. It is only in the silence of the mind that one can know oneself and also realize the purpose of life, if any. Indeed, this process of studying oneself quietly, while life flows on, is the only way to find peace.

Following a method prescribed by someone ultimately ends in collecting more and more concepts, more and more disciplines, beliefs, ideologies and finally, more and more frustration. To see clearly without any preconceived notions, precisely 'what-is' in the moment, itself turns into action, intuitive involuntary action, enormously satisfying.

Intellectual Elaboration

The very seal of truth of the doctrines of sages like Ramana Maharshi or Huang Po, compared with the extreme complexities of the religions into which each was born, is surely significant.

A philosophy, being an intellectual structure, evolves, whereas the teaching of Ramana Maharshi, being merely the conveying of spiritual experience, never varied over fifty years. And it is not a coincidence that the difference between Ramana Maharshi's teaching and the doctrine of Huang Po is merely a difference of terminology, not content.

When a brilliant disciple died, Ramana Maharshi was asked if this man of immense intellectual stature could have attained enlightenment in his lifetime. He is supposed to have replied: "How could he? His *sankalpas* – desires and ambitions, intellectuality and affectivity under the sway of the ego and its sense of personal doership – were too strong."

We observe little trace of intellectual elaboration and spiritual discipline in the doctrines of the founders of the great religions, and yet the great religions are highly complex and contentious in their developed forms. One would suppose that it is by no means easy to sift the recorded words attributed to the founders from those placed in their mouths several centuries later, but what appears authentic in the earliest recorded form has considerable simplicity, clearly absent from the others. This is so whether the teaching is attributed to Sri Krishna, the Buddha, or Jesus.

An obvious reason for such a happening could be that disciples who had appointed themselves as 'the leading ones', thinking they had perceived the truth of the doctrines – and yet *knew* that their understanding was not deep enough – had started elaborating the techniques into philosophies and disciplines in order to transmute their superficial understanding into realization.

Such methods, however, cannot succeed because the personal doership stands in the way as a massive obstruction. It is only when this is apperceived that the ultimate understanding can happen. The sense of personal doership in the ego cannot be eliminated by any act of will, nor can any discipline dispose of it, because all such attempts are clearly within its own plane – a thief posing as a policeman, as Ramana Maharshi put it.

The suppression of pride, ambition, guilt, and hatred cannot destroy their cause. An illness cannot be cured by suppressing the symptoms. The only way of elimination is to be able to accept *totally* that everything happens according to a Cosmic Law, and that no one is really capable of doing any deed or discipline.

This flash of total acceptance and transcendence can happen only through intuitive apprehension of the Divine Will as the basis of all happening.

Who Am I?

Ramana Maharshi's response to a query from Swami Nityabodhananda was: "You asked me if any difference exists between the 'normal' state of ordinary people and that of men who are 'realized'. The point is what have they realized? Only that which is real in themselves. But that which is real in them is equally real in you. Where is the difference?"

That which is not real is the sense of doership in the ego – the mind – the outgoing mind conceptualizing and objectivizing all the time. As Huang Po has pointed out in an impressive statement of utmost significance: "You cannot use mind to seek something from mind. Mind and the object of its search are one."

Where do these statements point if not 'within'? The more you think, the more you conceptualize, the further without you go. We are already there, 'within', wherein lies the 'Kingdom of Heaven' of Jesus.

The Maharshi has reiterated that at no time in his life had he practiced any kind of spiritual discipline, any *sadhana*, and nor was such practice necessary. Doing meditation without any expectation, but because you like it, is not *sadhana*. Why should any effort be necessary in order to enter into this 'I' that is your normal state? You only have to see clearly the hypnotic spell in which your abnormal state holds you, remain calm, and you are *what you really are*.

The personality that results from the genes and the environmental conditioning from conception to death – the ego – is necessarily the product of percepts and concepts. Thus, being a three-dimensional product, such personality cannot but partake of the unreality and impermanence of everything that belongs to that plane of appearance.

All that is necessary to realize is that such a personality – the ego – simply cannot be the doer of any deed, and that there is really no deed at all but a happening. When the ego has realized that no one can be the doer – neither 'me' nor the 'other' – and the thinking mind is held in abeyance, without any conceptualizing about the future, then living in the present moment, accepting whatever the moment brings – sometimes pain, sometimes pleasure – becomes simple: witnessing whatever happens, blaming neither oneself nor the 'other'.

Observing Without An Observer

Very few ever realize the value of Self-knowledge. Self-knowledge is the peace and tranquility that one seeks as the most important thing in life, whether one is aware of it or not. It cannot be sought as an intellectual pursuit, something of academic interest. It must necessarily be based on observing ourselves without any image of ourselves, wanting to be this or that. Our usual perception is not only with the senses but also with a heavily conditioned mind, resulting in a limited, partial perception.

It is only when one is able to see things without the preconceived notions of the 'me-observer' that one knows the immensity of what is observed. 'What-is' is a living thing that past knowledge and conditioning cannot possibly recognize. The matter is simple: where there is an observer as separate from what is observed, there can only be conflict. Real seeing means total observing without an observer recording it in memory.

Peace Of Mind

We hold onto a core belief that peace of mind can come from adequate achievements in the external world, irrespective of what the wise say. We become so busy worrying about providing for the future, and being resentful about those who we believe have stood in our way, that we put ourselves in the ridiculous situation of being at the mercy of the 'other'.

Truly, our peace of mind depends entirely on ourselves: how we react to events. If I am hurt in any way – physical, psychological or financial – and my reaction is that it is my destiny – God's Will, Cosmic Law – then the individual through which this happened is really irrelevant.

There is a radical change when life is perceived as a happening and not something done by anyone. However, in our daily living we must continue to accept whatever society decides about our actions, and their consequences. But we are free of any guilt or shame for our actions, as well as any hatred and malice.

'Enlightenment' is misconceived by many as awareness of more subtle dimensions, more energies, more powers – something beyond one's everyday mundane perceptions. I am now of the clear understanding that enlightenment obviously means seeing the same *samsara* in a different perspective altogether: everything is a happening, and there is no individual doer of any deed.

Universal Brotherhood

Do the terms 'ananda', 'divine love' and 'universal brotherhood' mean anything to the common man? It is not really difficult to understand and to accept that the term 'love', with its inherent possessivity, its sensuality, can only be the refraction in a denser medium of that which can be understood as *peace and harmony*. This can be seen in the daily living of some few people each of us know and recognize as a 'sage', a 'kind man', a 'wise man'.

It is easy to appreciate that this divine 'love' or 'peace and harmony', manifesting in us through the ego-doer, gets polluted by all the desires and avidities of that ego-doer, becomes affective, and acquires a heavy shadow that never leaves it.

We may be tired of hearing that 'what-is' on the plane of Reality has become what 'exists' on the plane of appearance, that the One has become the many.

Anyhow, it is a concept, an intellectual conception. This intellectual understanding can be transmuted into a deeper intuitional acceptance only if the concept is tested in the fire of one's own experience, piecemeal in daily living, instead of *en bloc*. It is necessary to investigate and analyze what we consider our conscious deeds, and find out if what we consider our action was indeed our action. It could not be our conscious action if it depended for its happening on the happening of an earlier event over which one had absolutely no control. For instance, if I find from my analysis of a particular action that if I had not had a particular thought, my action would not have happened – and I, of course, had no control over the happening of that thought.

Similarly, I would notice that if I had not *happened* to be at a particular place and time, and seen something, or heard, smelt, tasted, or touched something, what I consider my action would not have happened.

During the course of this analysis and investigation, it is more than likely that a flash of total understanding and acceptance would *happen*: I simply cannot be the doer of any action, and therefore, no one can be the doer of any action either!

We would then apperceive that everything *happens* in life, according to the Cosmic Law, and how anything affects anyone depends entirely on their destiny. Everything happens: no one to blame for anything.

And the absence of blame is the basis of *ananda*, divine love and universal brotherhood.

Removal Of A Barrier

Enlightenment is not the attainment or achieving of anything whatsoever. It is merely the removal of a barrier – the concept of the 'me' as an individual doer. Therefore, enlightenment is not enlightenment of 'myself'.

Nothing happens to anything. Mind plays no role in enlightenment.

Enlightenment is just the recovery of clear vision. It is purely a subjective adjustment without any objective existence. A sudden apperception that there is no 'me' doing anything in time. It is dying to the concept of dying.

YOGI IMPRESSIO

(Please fill all the details, in CAPITAL letter

☐ Join our free mailing list and receive informa
Or, fill up the on-line mailing list form on ou

☐ I am currently on your mailing list. Please co

Name: ☐ Mr. ☐ Ms._____

First Name

Address: ☐ Home ☐ Office_____

_____

Pin Code_____State_____

Company Name_____J

Tel: (Home)_____(Off.)_____

E-mail_____

Yogi Impressions Books Pvt. Ltd. 61, Anjali, Minoo Desai Road, Col
Tel: 91 (22) 22842923/4/6 Fax: 91 (22) 22046825 E-mail: yogi@yo
Website: www.yogiimpressions.com

Who Is This 'Me'?

When I ask myself 'What is time?', I have no definitive answer, though I *know* what it is. Similarly, when
the question arises: 'Who is this 'me'?', perhaps the only
real response is that the 'me' is what 'you' are not. And
yet both cannot be basically different. They are separate
entities only in relationship to one another in daily living.

Our sense of self is derived from the various aspects
which distinguish us as individuals – our relative
appearance, role in work and play, social and financial
status, and what others think of us. We also form our
identity from conditioning, which includes our beliefs and
values, education, and personal experience in life.

We derive our uniqueness as the individual
experiencer. But the essence of our being can only be
known when we are *not* the experiencer, and this is the
same for me and you. When the individual experiencer
is absent, and the mind is vacant, we cannot but be
aware of our essence as pure Consciousness. When the
'me', the individual entity, is absent as the one who is
conscious, then there is only Consciousness. This core of
one's being has none of the individual's uniqueness of
existence as the body-mind organism. There is only
Awareness of Being.

What Am I?

Am I God? No.
Am I the devil? No.
Am I an angel? No.
Am I a saint? No.
Then what am I?
I am Awareness.

69

In Your Own Interests

If you are selfish, what you will get is some kind of momentary pleasure or gain, which can only last a short while until the next moment that brings pain. Living means facing life from moment to moment, never knowing what the future will bring.

What you really need in life – whether you know it or not – is to be anchored in peace. You will not get it by being selfish.

The only way to get it is by always having a harmonious relationship with the 'other'. Being selfish may bring you some pleasure, but it has within itself the sense of guilt which prevents total contentment. Why accept fleeting pleasure at the cost of a deeper sense of peace?

Acceptance by a sage that his own body and personality have both good points and bad points, means 'humility' in himself accompanied by 'tolerance' for the 'other'.

However, if one insists on attaining perfection, it would be best to remember that perfection happens not when there is nothing more to be added, but when there is nothing more to be taken away.

The Negative Way

The major significance of non-doership is that it leads to the feeling of being anchored in peace and harmony while facing life from moment to moment. Are sages always comfortable with themselves and with other people? Well, they are never uncomfortable with themselves, and they are never uncomfortable with others. This is the negative way.

Seeing In The Now

The human being does not realize that one does not need time in one's life, because life really happens in the present moment. It is our mistaken notion, reinforced by the religions and evolutionary pundits, that we need time to evolve and fulfill ourselves, to change from 'what-is' to 'what-should-be'.

Time is certainly necessary in the realm of learning, achieving, and to earn a living by becoming proficient in some profession. But in the world of the psyche, we follow the old traditional pattern, and become frustrated and miserable when the hope of fulfillment is not achieved.

One becomes habituated to the conditioning of needing time for evolving into something other than what one is. However, a person who relies on horizontal time as a means to gain happiness or realize the Truth is deceiving himself. There is no understanding in time: it is now or never. What there is, is now. There is no never. Seeing the 'what-is' is always immediate. Truth is beyond reason and calculation. The observer can only be in the past or the future. The nature and futility of horizontal time is seen when the *seeing is in the now* without the seer.

Permanent Seeing

True seeing – permanent seeing – is seeing that one cannot see the absence of thought – which is Subjectivity.

Being is revealed – not to any one – at the point when sleep has not yet happened and external wakefulness vanishes. We cannot know it: we *are* it.

Persons Of Wisdom

Persons of wisdom, irrespective of their personal convictions or beliefs, seem to have a common denominational quality or characteristic – an unmistakable state of profound silence and stillness, an indelible mark of freedom and Self-knowledge, a deep-rooted humility and tolerance for the 'other'. A certain something, not particularly tangible, that draws people to them, wanting to be in their company. The basis of this attraction is the lack of stability and quietude of the average human mind. It is one's common experience that even when one is not engaged in doing something, one's mind is not silent or still. One talks to oneself – thinking about the past, present or future – sometimes actually uttering words without producing audible sounds. One also sees images while one's eyes are closed, entertaining ideas about persons, things and events.

A man is generally regarded as holy and superior when he lives in an ashram, praying the whole day, doing some gardening or charitable work, concerned all the time with self-control, self-discipline, self-castigation. On the other hand, we regard as an ordinary man, 'just like us', one who is always busy trying to earn money in his particular occupation or business. But is there essentially any difference between them? Both their minds are occupied – what they are occupied with is not important.

The mind of the man of wisdom, when not occupied with doing something specific in the present moment, remains free of the usual continuous chattering, and is vacant. An occupied mind can never penetrate into its own depth, into the untrodden spaces. It is this emptiness, says J. Krishnamurti, which gives space to the mind, in which time cannot enter. And out of this vacancy and emptiness arises creation.

Dreams

What happens in a dream? We observe ourselves as doing something. There is an ego, a separate entity, who thinks he is perceiving whatever seems to take place, but we know that it is we who perceive both the dream-ego and what is happening in the dream. The dream-ego is obviously a part of the whole scenario of the dream, and is as much real or unreal as any other element.

Our waking-ego cannot be any different. He may think that he perceives whatever is taking place as an independent spectator – like the dream-ego – but, again, he cannot be any more or less real than any other element in the scenario of daily living. It is only the real 'I' who is the real spectator of the dream that is taking place as daily living, and that 'I' is the impersonal 'I'.

That there is actually no difference between waking life and dream life is what Chuang Tzu was demonstrating when he said that, having dreamt that he was a butterfly flitting from flower to flower, on waking, he wondered whether he then had been a man dreaming he was a butterfly, or might not now be a butterfly dreaming he was a man.

Adequate Action

There is no action on the plane of Being. Non-action on the plane of Being becomes, on the plane of existing, correct action, which may range from inaction to even violence.

The Taoist doctrine of non-action is based on the understanding that what we regard as action is in fact the reaction of our artificial, superficial ego to external events, happenings: we really do not act. We human beings are obsessed with the necessity of *doing* something, literally terrified of the possibility of inaction, glorifying and admiring doers, regardless of the havoc they might have caused. We usually forget that inaction in certain circumstances may have a dynamic quality, which requires vision and self-control.

We are brought up to believe that in all circumstances we should be doing something: rather than face the possibility of having nothing to do, we spend time drinking alcohol or consuming drugs. We simply do not know how *to be*.

Action that is correct can only be spontaneous action: the product of the split-second that outwits the frame of time. Correct action can, therefore, only be that action that has happened through the ego that has no longer any sense of personal doership. Any action based on positive or negative affectivity, not natural or genuine, is unlikely to be correct. Similarly, action based on relative reasoning or memory is also not likely to be correct because such action would be a reaction.

It must also be clearly understood that correct action would not necessarily mean *successful* action in worldly terms.

Perhaps correct action could be best described as adequate action, no more than is needed in the circumstances.

Terrorism And War

Whatever happens in the world is perceived in opposite ways. Most people, who viewed on TV the 9/11 incident in New York, would have been horrified at the destruction caused by the two planes ramming into the buildings. But, for the perpetrators of the act, the scene must have sent them into raptures. It is not difficult to imagine Osama Bin Laden and his comrades falling on their knees and thanking Allah for the enormous damage done by the act. They probably expected about 40-50 people, rather than 5000 people, to be injured or dead.

The point is that the basis of the manifestation, and its functioning that we call life, is the existence, at any moment, of both the interconnected opposites of every conceivable kind, beginning with male and female.

There never was a time when both were not present. To want one without the other – only the beautiful, not the ugly; only the good, not the evil – always choosing, means not accepting the basic *duality* of life. This is living life in *dualism*, and this results in frustration and unhappiness.

Therefore *devas* and *rakshasas* (gods and demons) have always been at each other's throats – sometimes one is on top, sometimes the other. Each one has a 'cause'!

Guard Yourself

No harm could possibly come to me through holding myself to be less than someone else, even if it is not so. But I must guard myself from holding myself superior to others, even if they be the greatest sinners.

Desire For Security

We are so used to authority and guidance that we forget that this urge springs from the fear of insecurity.

Our desire is not only for material security but, even more, for psychological security. It is this desire to reach some end, which leads to the acceptance of guidance, the worship of success, looking for leaders, masters and gurus.

This urge is the outcome of being insecure, the desire to find something permanent in the impermanence of life.

The result is that we take flight into known beliefs and rituals, the comforting formulae of religious teachers, and reassurances of priests. So the fear of the unknown continues to rule our lives.

Our real freedom would, therefore, be the freedom from the known – being open and receptive to the unknown, instead of being afraid of it. Freedom must be in the negation of the past with its discipline, tradition, and restrictive authority.

Such freedom could give rise to the end of conceptualizing, horizontal thinking – the awakening into a state of *jivanmukta*, described in the *Bhagavad Gita* as one who is liberated while living his life – liberated from the confines of the thinking mind, hatred for oneself, and malice for the 'other'.

Nothing More

When will I have everything? Only when I want nothing more. This means, in effect, peace with myself and harmony with the 'other' – which is the absence of the 'me', the presence of I AM. This is the approach of negation.

Forget About The Results

Lord Krishna, in the *Bhagavad Gita*, says: "The world is imprisoned in its own activity, except when actions are performed as worship of God. Therefore, you must perform every action sacramentally, and be free from all attachment to results. You have the right to work, but for the sake of work only. You have no rights to the fruits of work. Desire for the fruits of work must never be your motive in working. They who work selfishly for results are miserable."

That so much has been said in the *Bhagavad Gita* is a measure of the importance of the subject. The pity of it, however, is that what has been said is grievously misinterpreted. For this reason, most modern men and women find this quotation not only unacceptable but quite incomprehensible.

These verses are misinterpreted as being asked to work without motivation. This is quite incorrect. What is said plainly is to do your work at any time as best as you can, decide what you want in any given situation, which is your motivation, and put in any kind of effort that you choose. This is your right, your free will. But having done this much, remember that your lifetime experience – and everyone's experience – is that what actually happens, the fruits of your action have never been in your control. If you keep your mind and heart on the results, you will be miserable.

Thus, the advice in the *Bhagavad Gita* should be interpreted as doing at any time whatever you want to do *well*, but after you have done it, remember that the outcome has never been in your control. Therefore, having finished one job, do not keep waiting for the fruits. Take up the next job and the next... Results will keep happening according to God's Will – Cosmic Law. Forget about the results. Otherwise you will not be able to concentrate on the next job, and you will be frustrated.

Motivation there is, but only before you decide what to do. Once you have done what you wanted to do, the question of motivation does not arise.

One cannot leave the *Bhagavad Gita* without acknowledging the following quotations of Lord Krishna: "There never was a time when I did not exist nor you... nor is there any future in which we shall cease to be."

Obviously, 'we' could not refer to the individual separate entities in these particular circumstances, but similar characters in similar situations.

Finally: "That which is non-existent can never come into existence, and that which is, can never cease to be."

Perfection

The deeper the understanding goes, the fewer words it needs for the necessary expression. That is how one presumes the Upanishadic statements came about. The pronouncements seem to have an authentic intensity about them.

Perfection is attained not when nothing more can be added, but when nothing more can be taken away. When an image is being hewn out of a piece of stone, the sculptor keeps chipping away until he cannot cut any more. Then the image is ready.

Virtue

Man's seeking is based on the principle of pleasure as opposed to pain, physical or psychological. This pursuit of pleasure happens at even a subtle level. Even when religious people say that they are seeking truth or God, the seeking is still based on the principle of pleasure as opposed to pain. The pleasure is not necessarily only sensuous pleasure. There can be, when there is a little refinement, a little more culture, the pleasure of reformation, the pleasure of giving, the pleasure of doing good, of making the world a better place.

The particular kind of pleasure one seeks would depend to a very large extent on one's programming – genes plus conditioning – but nonetheless the activity as such would still be based on the constant demand for greater and greater satisfaction.

Thus we find, from our own life and living, that what we call 'virtue' is still based on the demand for pleasure.

So what? Should we stop our activity? That is just the point. One does not have to *do* anything. Merely seeing – and understanding life and living – shows us that whatever is happening is just that: a *happening* and not the *doing* by any individual entity.

To understand the hidden urges and compulsions – to be clearly aware of them, without any judgment – means freedom: freedom of suffering from guilt and shame. It means the denial of everything one thought one has been. Indeed, such seeing is itself the most positive action, without any doing.

Man And Actor

As Shakespeare has said: "All the world's a stage, and all the men and women merely players." Ramana Maharshi often referred to this metaphor comparing man and actor: "All the actions that a body is to perform are already decided upon at the time it comes into existence: the only freedom you have is whether to identify yourself with the body."

The role of the human being as an actor is cast the moment he comes onto the stage of manifestation – the moment he is born – and he has to play it out precisely as it is written according to God's Will or the Cosmic Law. But while he is being an actor, doing his role, he remains an independent separate entity, witnessing actions happening. Of course, his apparent freedom remains in whether – again according to the Cosmic Law – he chooses to remember his basic identity as one three-dimensional object in the manifestation or whether he considers himself an independent doer of his actions.

As has been said by Wei Wu Wei: "David Garrick plays Othello or Romeo, Falstaff or Botham, and identifies himself with the part. He has been such a good actor precisely because he does that. He loves and hates, saves and slays, laughs and weeps – he lives the life of that character – but his part was decreed by Shakespeare. He plays the role again and again and varies his interpretation, but he cannot depart from the text. But he is David Garrick all the time. David Garrick is the reality, Othello or Falstaff, the role in the play. Perhaps waiting in the wings in between he is aware that he is David Garrick, then when his cue comes he identifies again with the personage."

An actor plays his role better when he relies on his God-given genius and on his technique, rather than on his personal doership. Similarly, it is often seen that a man plays his part in life better when he ceases to identify himself with the psychosomatic apparatus as the thinker, doer, experiencer, and identifies himself as a mere apparatus through which the Primal Energy functions and brings about whatever is to happen through that programmed apparatus, according to God's Will.

Life As A Movie

Can the human being be anything more real than a cinema film? When the light in the projector is switched off, what can remain but the screen? What was projected by the light was no more than a series of stills, a series of frames. Is what is projected by life any different than a series of projections from moment to moment, connected by memory into a series of causes and effects? What has been happening is that we have not been able to conceive of 'ourselves' as projections, which we have been mistaking for reality. Such a concept could perhaps lead us to an awareness that would open the way to the ultimate understanding, the necessary intuitional cognition that transcends all concepts.

The TV Serial Of Life

How do we live our lives? Despite knowing that our actions are what we are compelled to do, and not what we *thought* we should do – because we simply cannot do otherwise – we continuously praise and blame ourselves and the 'other' for what actually happened.

Furthermore, we accept the whole social and political structure that is based on the absurdity that one has always had freedom to do whatever he wants and is responsible for each action.

Supposing, as suggested by Wei Wu Wei, we were to *realize* and *live* what we know intellectually, in every hour and detail of our lives – then it would seem that we were not living our lives, but merely watching a TV serial.

Who Cares?!

Who are we? What are we? Whatever one says would be a concept – and a concept can never be the truth. We are what we are. I am what I am. You are what you are. Physically, psychologically, financially. Neither of us has any control over anything.

All that we can do in life is to witness whatever is happening through anyone. No one is doing anything and no one can be blamed for anything. Everything happens. Society, of course, continues to judge everything and its verdict has to be accepted.

This should not be too difficult. Who am I? What is the purpose of life? Who cares?! Flippant? Maybe, but this is as near to the Truth as anything can be.

Do I Have Free Will?

I certainly have free will, if by free will I understand that, in any given situation, I can do whatever I think I should do. But the fact of the matter is that my free will does not make the slightest difference to the happening of life. It simply means that I can decide what I want and make the necessary effort to try and achieve my goal.

But my lifetime experience is that what actually happens would be sometimes what I wanted, sometimes not what I wanted, and at others what I did not want.

Then again, I come to an interesting revelation when I examine the basis of my free will. I find, from my personal experience, that my free will depends almost entirely on two factors, over neither of which I had any influence at all: my genes and the conditioning that I have been continuously exposed to – at home, in school, society, church, or temple.

What then is the conclusion? It is that I do have free will to do whatever I think I should in any given situation, but that I have totally no control over what happens or over the consequences of the happening. What seems to be 'my' free will is actually God's Will.

God makes me do 'His' will and makes me think that it is 'my' will. Is that not a real joke?

All I Need

This is so obvious that it is almost funny: whatever I have is all I need, what God has given me, to reach the goal for which He created me.

How can we know that the world is transitory, that time is passing, that nothing stands still? We cannot know that our river is flowing unless we have one foot on the bank! There is no entity, only a continuum, and that continuum is Consciousness.

Stillness In Movement

T'ai Chi, the ancient martial art form, is essentially about movements, but it is also concerned with the principles behind them – to discover the stillness in the movement and the energy that flows. Bending your knees to sink lower is a T'ai Chi technique which stems from training for combat. Sinking lower allows you to root more firmly to the ground. This happens to be a behavioral characteristic of natural humility.

An anecdote, reputed to be an actual happening, reflects this. When the party started moving from the drawing room to the dining table, two people, who obviously knew each other well, happened to come to a narrow opening at the same time. One of them stood his full height and pronounced: "I never let my inferiors precede me." The other one bent himself slightly, gestured to the first to proceed, and said: "I always do."

As the Tao Te Ching observes: "All rivers run to the sea because it is lower than they are. The ocean's willingness to be humbler and lower than the rivers gives it its power."

Watchfulness

An excellent way to meditate is to observe your mind silently, without any judgment, without any explanation. If you just allow the mind to be aware of its own struggle and confusion, you will find the mind arriving at a state in which struggle has given way to a beautiful watchfulness that is astonishingly peaceful. And even more astounding will be that the ego-seeker has nothing to do with it.

A Natural Occurrence

It is only when true meditation happens that one realizes the incredible beauty of the event and sympathizes with those who have not tasted it.

This is not to suggest that everyone must learn to meditate! An enquiring mind perhaps would inevitably come to it because it is such a natural occurrence – the 'what-is', Self-knowing, Self-realization.

Meditation is not something to be achieved. It requires, as part of one's programming, a deep sensitivity. It cannot be cultivated, induced or disciplined. Someone programmed differently would in all probability consider meditation a waste of time into escapism!

I Am Awareness

I am Awareness itself – impersonal awareness,
neither 'me' nor the 'other'.
Knowing this, first I gave up action.
Events happen. No one does any deed.
When I gave up action, I found
I had already given up idle words, idle thinking.
All things arise, suffer change and pass away.
This is Nature.
Knowing I am Awareness itself,
how can there be any thinking
about what I have done or left undone?
I become Stillness.

Still Mind

Where the mind is concerned, the all-important point is whether it is still or occupied. It is only in a still mind, that one's real nature can be discovered. What the mind is occupied with is of no real significance.

We are conditioned to regard as a holy and extraordinary man, one who prays all day, does innocuous work such as gardening for a living, whose mind is wholly occupied with God, self-discipline, self-control, sin, and guilt. On the other hand, we consider as an ordinary man not worth bothering about, the one who is busy all day working in the office and is always concerned with making money.

With this conditioning we do not realize the value of being still. This does not mean doing no action. One can be in meditation and yet not have a still mind. One can be engaged in one's job, paying attention to the work that is being done, and yet have a still mind.

A still mind is the one in which conceptualizing is not happening in horizontal time, irrespective of whatever the body-mind organism may be doing in the moment.

Key To Freedom

The key to freedom is a state of intense attention, deep awareness, free from accumulated conditioning. It cannot be purchased through discipline, practice or anything else. It can only happen when the mind is free of accumulated knowledge and desire for more knowledge.

The Core Of The Bhagavad Gita Teaching

The core of the *Bhagavad Gita* teaching comprises a remarkable combination of *karma-yoga*, *bhakti-yoga* and *jnana-yoga*.

The *Gita* does not advise anyone to take to *sanyasa* for the simple reason that it recognizes that, in most cases, it turns out to be only an escape from life. Instead, the *Gita* asks the householder to put in his best efforts in his work, whatever it is, without any sense of doership, without hankering for expected results, which means frustration. This is *karma-yoga*.

He must live his life never forgetting God at any moment. This is *bhakti-yoga*.

If the householder has an enquiring mind, it is suggested that while he is living his life, diligently doing his daily work – without thinking of the expected results – with faith in God, he should turn his mind towards the enquiry into Truth – Knowledge. This is *jnana-yoga*.

The Happening

Somewhere, somehow, something happens; it has an effect. Someone is greatly benefited and friendship or love are created. Somewhere, somehow, something happens; it has an effect. Someone is badly hurt, physically, psychologically or financially – enmity or hatred happens.

This is life and daily living. Isn't life crazy? Isn't life funny? Life flows – and needs no reason for any happening.

What Is Faith?

There is no faith in God without total acceptance of 'what-is' in the present moment – including all the ugliness.

Embracing Nature

Ultimate understanding has not happened until one is supremely confident that there would be wholehearted participation in the rejoicing and celebration of nature, even if a huge earthquake were to occur the very next moment.

Cosmic Law

Equidistant from the atoms and the stars, our exploratory horizons are being expanded to embrace both the very small and the very large. With a universe that is expanding with no edge in space, no beginning or end in time, it would seem that everything is going according to a Cosmic Law, and there is nothing more for the Creator to do.

Why?

A painting can never know why its painter created it.

One With God

Have I become one with God through reading books,
through writing books, through meditation, through good
deeds, through prayers? No, only through God Himself.
No, not even that. God has made me one with Him.

Final Understanding

You are not the doer of any deed.
Whatever you think and do at any time is dictated by
your programming – genes and environmental
conditioning – which God created.
Thus you cannot make a mistake.
You cannot commit a sin.
Everything is a happening, not any deed done by anyone.
God made all things. There is only God.
Was anything more to be said at any time?

The Sage: A Man Of Wisdom

The sage, a man of wisdom, is a symbol of that mysterious virtue and supernal simplicity; a messenger of peace and harmony, a herald of humility.

His own daily living is a striking testimony of the practicality of his basic concepts that might seem at first sight to be idealistic but impractical.

His daily talks take place regularly with such apparent ease and flow, and there is no one to claim any merit.

The sage never magnifies himself; thus he becomes perfect in his greatness. He seems to do all things silently, mysteriously, effectively.

His teaching – his 'set of concepts' – is so marvelous in its immaculate simplicity that those who find it and delight in it, often times do not know it because they are like little children. While those who seek it, do not find it because their minds are not vacant like those of little children, but full of proud learning.

In the sage's daily living there is much to suggest the ebb and flow, the action and interaction, of existence and non-existence, of the higher and the lower, of the inner and the outer, of the strong and the weak, of the positive and the negative, of the full and the empty, of the expansion and the contraction – all this with great felicity, as there is no implication of dualism. There is the total acceptance of the underlying unity between the unmanifest and the manifest, between the deep understanding and the daily living.

⤙

The sage accomplishes a great deal, but does not identify himself with the deed nor with its merit, but retires into himself and abides in peace and serenity.

⤙

The sage is never unaware that the soft and the hard, the strong and the weak, and all such opposites, are the essential elements of the duality of manifestation and its functioning that we know as 'life'. Therefore, the sage recognizes his utter dependence on the Divine, and his strength is perfected in weakness.

⤙

The sage does not lay up treasure: his riches are within. The more he gives to others, the more he has of his own. He is considerate of the ideas of others, never forgetting the essential unities. He lives in the world, yet remains withdrawn. He lives in accord with mankind, yet remains himself.

⤙

The sage has three treasures to which he holds fast: compassion, economy and humility. Through compassion he shows courage; through economy he can give freely to others; through humility he becomes a 'vessel of the highest honor'.

The sage, being fully aware that 'love' and 'hate' are both based on what the 'other' has done, and therefore really do not exist, lives his daily life accepting whatever each happening brings in the moment – sometimes pain, sometimes pleasure – as something supposed to happen according to the Cosmic Law. His relationship with the 'other' is therefore always harmonious, and this leads to his own constant peace of mind.

Mind's essential peace is disturbed when the deeper meaning of life is not understood. Everything is a happening according to the Cosmic Law, which is concerned with the entire universe for all eternity. There is no action done by any individual entity. When this is understood, there is peace and harmony. The sage does not try to achieve passivity by stopping activity, having realized that the very effort itself generates activity.

The mind of the sage exists undisturbed in the Way of the Cosmic Law, without any trace of 'this or that', 'right or wrong'. Nothing is taken personally, and thus nothing can offend any longer. Peace and harmony prevails.

It is distinctly noticeable that the sage, in his daily living, seems to do his routine work not only effortlessly but extremely efficiently. This is really not difficult to understand. The 'thinking mind' of the sage being absent, the 'working mind' of the sage is not hampered by illusory fears creating unnecessary problems in an illusory future. When the thinking-objects vanish, the thinking-subject also vanishes.

After the ultimate understanding has happened, the sage suddenly realizes, with a certain amount of surprise, that to have been attached to the idea of enlightenment was the obstacle. Enlightenment is not an achievement, not an end in itself. It is a happening which brings peace and harmony to the entity concerned, who continues to face the rest of his life from moment to moment.

The sage realizes how astonishingly simple and innocent is that which at one time seemed such an insurmountable impasse: the problem of bondage, freedom and enlightenment. It is so obvious. Each separate entity obeys its own nature conferred upon it by God: over this, it has no choice. It is impossible for any puny human brain to understand God's Will. Where is the question of right and wrong? Every happening will have its own consequence, be it happiness or unhappiness. It is the burdensome practice of judging that brings weariness, and prevents the acceptance of 'what-is' in the moment.

The sage has understood that enlightenment does not mean escaping from the world of senses and ideas, but participating in it totally with peace and equanimity. He strives to no goal.

The sage is aware that his happiness, his peace of mind, does not depend upon what others think of him. He understands that those whose programming – genes and conditioning – resonates with his own body-mind organism may 'like' him, while others may not. He is not really concerned with either.

It is said that awakening is always sudden, but deliverance gradual. 'Deliverance' happens for the unified mind, in accord with the Cosmic Law, when all self-centered striving ceases, doubts and irreconciliations vanish, and life flows in all innocence.

Nothing clings to the sage, and the sage clings to nothing. In his world of 'amness' and 'suchness', there is neither the self nor the other-than-self to be concerned with the unreality of life. The sage rests in perfect harmony with his mantra: Only a happening, never a doer.

The sage is certainly aware of his ego as a separate entity. However, because of the absence of a sense of personal doership, there is such a deep sense of withdrawal that when he hears anything said about him, his immediate reaction is: "Who, me?!"

Index

BOOKS BY RAMESH S. BALSEKAR

The Seeking (2004)

The Happening of a Guru: A Biography (2003)

Confusion No More (2003)

Guru Pournima (2003)

Peace and Harmony in Daily Living (2003)

The Ultimate Understanding (2001)

Advaita, the Buddha and the Unbroken Whole (2000)

It So Happened That... The Unique Teaching
of Ramesh S. Balsekar (2000)

Sin and Guilt: Monstrosity of Mind (2000)

Meaningful Trivialities from the Source (2000)

The Infamous Ego (1999)

Who Cares?! (1999)

The Essence of the Bhagavad Gita (1999)

Your Head in the Tiger's Mouth (1997)

Consciousness Writes (1996)

A Net of Jewels (1996)

The Bhagavad Gita – A Selection (1995)

Like a Large Immovable Rock (1994)

Ripples (1994)

Consciousness Speaks (1992)

From Consciousness to Consciousness (1989)

The Final Truth (1989)

A Duet of One (1989)

Experiencing the Teaching (1988)

Explorations into the Eternal (1987)

Experience of Immortality (1984)

Pointers from Nisargadatta Maharaj (1982)

For information on Ramesh Balsekar visit:
www.rameshbalsekar.com

For further details, contact:
Yogi Impressions Books Pvt. Ltd.
61, Anjali, Minoo Desai Road, Colaba,
Mumbai 400 005, India.
Website: www.yogiimpressions.com

Telephone: (022) 22842923/4/6
Fax: (022) 22046825
E-mail: yogi@yogiimpressions.com

Also visit:
www.indiayogi.com

Spiritual Resources from India

ALSO PUBLISHED BY YOGI IMPRESSIONS

Paperback

The Seeking
by Ramesh Balsekar

Here's a taste of a modern sage's daily talks, over three days, with visitors from all over the world, who gather at his residence in Mumbai. Questions that intrigue seekers of the truth are answered, with insight and clarity, in Ramesh's typical free-flowing dialogues, laced with his delightful good humour.

Hardbound,
Art Paper, Colour

The Happening of a Guru
A biography of Ramesh S. Balsekar

This anecdotal biography offers glimpses of Ramesh growing up in the austere Saraswat Community. His career as a banker and his contact with Nisargadatta Maharaj, culminate in his becoming a modern-day guru and the foremost Advaita sage. Rare photographs of Ramesh and his family are the highlights of this book.

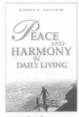
Paperback

Peace and Harmony in Daily Living
by Ramesh Balsekar

All the time, we find ourselves seeking something more in life. A modern sage points out that each of us, at some time or the other, has a taste of what it is: an uninterrupted experience of peace and harmony. He explains how to achieve this constant repose in ordinary, busy daily living. This is what the seeking – most evidently, the spiritual seeking – is all about.

Hardbound, Art Paper

The Ultimate Understanding
by Ramesh Balsekar

The complete essentials of the Hindu philosophy of Advaita or Non-duality, by a man who is recognised as one of the foremost contemporary Indian sages. This treasure of Advaita is unrivalled in its unique conceptual expression of the highest Truth, delivered with fundamental wisdom, simplicity and clarity.

Paperback

Stillness Speaks
by Eckhart Tolle

The essence of his teaching in short, simple pieces that everyone can understand. The book is arranged in ten chapters with subjects ranging from 'Beyond the Thinking Mind' to 'Suffering & the End of Suffering'. The result is a book filled with timely and powerful messages, and profoundly transformative when read as a whole.

Hardbound and Paperback

The Power of Now
by Eckhart Tolle
(Hindi Edition – Shaktiman Vartaman)

To make the journey into 'The Power of Now', you will need to leave your analytical mind and its false created self, the ego, behind. The journey is challenging, yet Eckhart Tolle describes it simply in a question and answer format to guide us. It is here, in the Now, you can find your joy and embrace your true self.

Paperback

Practicing The Power of Now
by Eckhart Tolle

This handy companion book to Eckhart Tolle's internationally bestselling 'The Power of Now' extracts the essence of his spiritual teaching. Arranged in it are a set of meditations and exercises to actually help you lead a more liberated life, and discover the path to "a life of grace, ease and lightness."

Paperback

Treasure Forest
by Cat Bordhi

A narrative adaptation of the spiritual teachings of Eckhart Tolle's 'The Power of Now'. Captivating characters and a highly suspenseful plot that presents one delightful surprise after another. Targeted for ages 10 and up, adults will also find it a highly memorable reading experience. Winner of the Nautilus Award for best Young Adult Fiction, '04.

Imported, Art Paper

Architects of Peace
by Michael Collopy

Nelson Mandela, Benazir Bhutto, Maya Lin, Pope John Paul II – 75 visionary men and women advocate their world-view for peace. Through their portraits and personal words, acclaimed photographer Michael Collopy demonstrates what the world's cultures can and must achieve in order to guarantee our future.

Imported, Hardbound,
Art Paper, Colour

The Buddha
Writings on the Enlightened One

A stunning 'visual biography' that collects excerpts from ancient texts to writings by Buddhist monks, religious scholars, literary luminaries and blends them with gorgeous photographs of Buddhism around the world by photographer Glen Allison. It's a collector's item.

Imported, Hardbound,
Art Paper, Colour

A Simple Monk
Writings on His Holiness The Dalai Lama

Replete with never-before published photographs by Alison Wright, it captures – through articles written by His mother Diki Tsering and renowned authors like Pico Iyer, Spalding Grey and Prof. Robert A. F. Thurman – the multi-dimensional personality of His Holiness The Dalai Lama.

Paperback

As You Think
by James Allen

One of the world's bestselling 'self-empowerment' books, it not only reveals that the keys to success are within our own minds, it shows us how to use these keys to unlock the greatest fulfilment we can imagine. A simple yet powerful reminder that "all we achieve and all that we fail to achieve is the direct result of our own thoughts."

Paperback

From Science to God
by Peter Russell

A physicist's journey into the mystery of consciousness, this book presents a new worldview in which science and spirit no longer conflict. The bridge between them, Russell shows, is light. He invites us to cross that bridge to a radically different, and ultimately healing, view of ourselves and the universe.

Paperback

Present Moment Awareness
by Shannon Duncan

'Present Moment Awareness' is filled with practical, down-to-earth advice for living in the present. With easy, accessible exercises, it shows readers how they can drop their emotional baggage, calm their worries about the future, and start enjoying the peace and happiness that can only be found in the present moment.

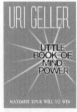
Pocketbook

Little Book of Mind-Power
by Uri Geller

Every page will energise you with a new confidence and determination to develop and super-charge your own will to win. Uri Geller teaches us how we can tap into the hidden strengths each one of us possesses and explore our highest individual potential.

Paperback

The Millionaire Course
by Marc Allen

The author became a multi-millionaire using the principles in this book. Here are 168 keys that will help you open the doors to success. Use the ones that resonate with your life experience. You'll discover that you can improve the quality of your life, and in the process improve the quality of the world around you.

Paperback

Stop Sleepwalking Through Life!
by Devdas Menon

Drawing inspiration from various spiritual traditions, Dr. Menon guides the reader through nine graded chapters to the full meaning of 'awareness'. He establishes that awakening and continual awareness of one's ego-self not only bring freedom from mind-made suffering, but also enhance the quality of one's work and one's life.

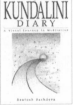

Paperback, Colour

Kundalini Diary
by Santosh Sachdeva

So much fear-mongering has been generated in average literature about the Kundalini, that this book comes as a great relief in the assertion of another possibility. In this volume, the author shows that the arousal of Kundalini can be a natural process and not one to be dreaded. In fact, the Kundalini can become a good, wise and loving friend.

Paperback, Colour

Conscious Flight into the Empyrean
by Santosh Sachdeva

A first-hand account of an extraordinary voyage into the subtle realms, this diary is a rare depiction of the visual unfolding of the Kundalini energy that challenges conventional views of perception and experience. It contains the author's own illustrations of the visions seen in her daily meditations.

Pocketbook

The Secret
by Áine Keenan

A contemplation in verse on the nature of Identity, Reality and Mystery. It possesses an appeal which is timeless and universal. This collection of poems is inspired by the teachings of the Advaita sage, Ramesh Balsekar.